MAP OF
MARYLAND

SHOWING
TEN COUNTIES AND THIRTY PARISHES AS LAID OUT IN 1692-1694
IN ACCORDANCE WITH THE LAW OF 1692 ESTABLISHING
THE CHURCH OF ENGLAND

AND ALSO SHOWING
THE LOCATIONS OF THE PRESENT CHURCHES OF THE STATE

COMPILED BY
PERCY G. SKIRVEN

TO ACCOMPANY
"THE FIRST PARISHES OF THE PROVINCE OF MARYLAND"

PUBLISHED BY
THE NORMAN, REMINGTON COMPANY, BALTIMORE

1923

DIOCESE OF MARYLAND	DIOCESE OF EASTON	DIOCESE OF WASHINGTON
Harford County, Maryland		
Baltimore " "	Cecil County, Maryland	District of Columbia
Baltimore City, "	Kent " "	Montgomery County, Maryland
Carroll County, "	Queen Annes County, Maryland	Prince George's " "
Howard " "	Talbot " "	Charles " "
Anne Arundel County, "	Caroline " "	St. Mary's " "
Calvert " "	Dorchester " "	
Frederick " "	Somerset " "	
Washington " "	Wicomico " "	
Alleghany " "	Worcester " "	
Garrett " "		

BISHOP'S RESIDENCE. UNIVERSITY PARKWAY, BALTIMORE

BISHOP'S RESIDENCE. EASTON MD

BISHOP'S RESIDENCE. MT. ST. ALBAN'S WASHINGTON D. C.

SYMBOLS

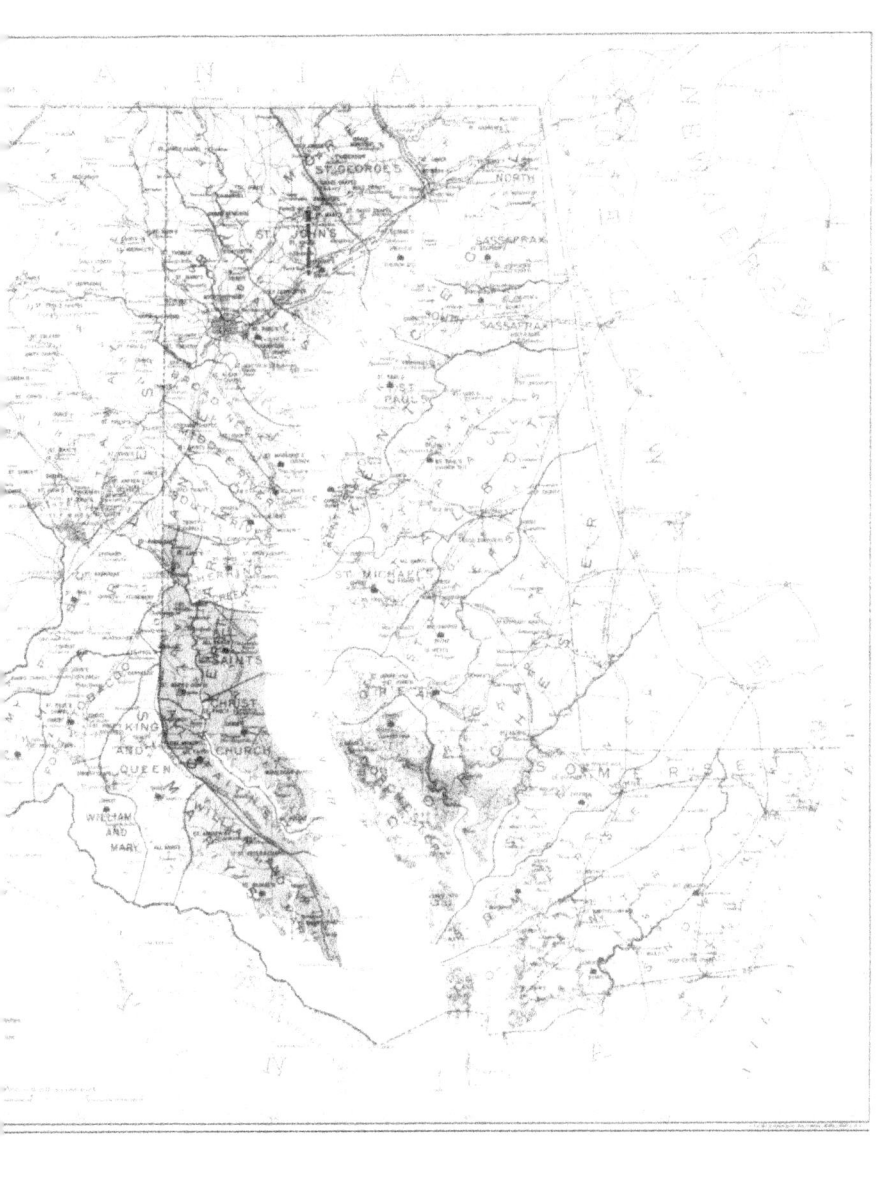

ISLE OF KENT

In 1631 Claiborne brought to the "Isle of Kent" from Hampton, Virginia, the Rev. Richard James, a minister of the Church of England, who conducted there in the virgin forest along the shores of Eastern Bay the first Christian Services held in the territory now within the bounds of Maryland.

THE FIRST PARISHES
Of the PROVINCE of
MARYLAND

Wherein are given HISTORICAL SKETCHES of the ten COUNTIES & of the thirty PARISHES in the PROVINCE at the time of the ❊ ❊ ESTABLISHMENT ❊ ❊ Of the CHURCH of ENGLAND In MARYLAND in 1692 ❊ ❊

ALSO
A Short Treatise On the Religious Situation In the Province Before the Establishment

Together With
56 ILLUSTRATIONS

By PERCY G. SKIRVEN

CLEARFIELD COMPANY

Copyright © 1923

Reprinted for
Clearfield Company, Inc. by
Genealogical Publishing Co., Inc.
Baltimore, Maryland
1994

International Standard Book Number 0-8063-4506-3

To the memory of my beloved son
THOMAS WILLIAM SKIRVEN,
whose sweet and sterling character
has ever been an inspiration,
this book is affectionately
dedicated.

CONTENTS

PART I	Historical Notes, 1634–1692..................	1– 19
PART II	Papers relating to Religious Conditions Prior to the Establishment	
	Queries about Maryland, 1676.................	23– 25
	Religious Conditions in the Province, 1676......	26– 27
	Meeting of the Lords of Trade and Plantation, 1677.....................................	28
	Lord Baltimore's Statement of Religious Conditions, 1677...............................	29– 30
	Lord Baltimore's Answers to the Queries about Maryland, 1678...........................	32– 34
	Address to King William, 1689................	35– 36
	Instructions to Gov. Lionel Copley, 1691........	37– 38
	Names of the Associators, 1690................	39
	Names of Council and Assemblymen, 1692......	40– 43
	Repeal of Former Laws.......................	44
PART III	First Law Establishing the Church of England, 1692.....................................	47– 58
	Taxables....................................	59
	Sheriffs' Jurisdiction..........................	60
PART IV	Instructions to Vestrymen.....................	63– 68
PART V	Law under which the Church Functioned for seventy Years.................................	71– 94
	Papers relating to the Validity of the above Law.	95– 97
	Disposition of the "Forty per Poll" Tax........	98–102
PART VI	Counties, Parishes, Hundreds, Churches, Vestrymen, Ministers, etc.........................	105–164
PART VII	Papers relating to the Establishment...........	165–167
	Acts of Assembly, 1698–1765.................	
	Census of Maryland, 1696....................	
	Parishes of Maryland and the District of Columbia, 1922.................................	
INDEX:	Names, Counties, Court Houses, Hundreds, Parishes, Churches, Geographical names and Miscellaneous Subjects.........................	
MAP	of the Province of Maryland, 1692 (also shows location of Churches in 1922).......................	

ILLUSTRATIONS

Church		County	Page
Isle of Kent	Kent Island	Queen Anne's	*Frontispiece*
St. Mary's River	St. Mary's City	St. Mary's	6
Old Oak Tree	St. Paul's Cemetery	Kent	15
Old Council House	Annapolis	Anne Arundel	62
County Seal		Kent	107
Trinity Church	St. Mary's City	St. Mary's	110
St. Andrew's Church	Leonardtown	St. Mary's	111
St. George's Church	Valley Lee	St. Mary's	112
Christ Church	Chaptico	St. Mary's	113
Emmanuel Church	Chestertown	Kent	114
Vestry House	St. Paul's Church	Kent	115
Christ Church	Stevensville	Queen Anne's	116
St. Paul's Church	Fairlee	Kent	117
State House	Annapolis	Anne Arundel	118
St. James' Church	Herring Creek	Anne Arundel	120
All Hallows Church	South River	Anne Arundel	121
St. Ann's Church	Annapolis	Anne Arundel	122
St. Margaret's Church	Westminster	Anne Arundel	123
Middleham Chapel	Lusby	Calvert	124
St. Paul's Church	Prince Frederick	Calvert	125
Christ Church	Port Republic	Calvert	126
All Saints Church	Sunderland	Calvert	127
St. Paul's Church	Baden	Prince George's	128
All Faiths Church	Mechanicsville	St. Mary's	129
St. Paul's Church	Rock Creek	District of Columbia	130
Christ Church	Wayside	Charles	132
Christ Church	La Plata	Charles	133
Christ Church	Grayton	Charles	134
St. John's Church	Broad Creek	Prince George's	135
All Saints' Church	Frederick	Frederick	136
Rectory	St. Paul's Parish	Baltimore City	137
Vestry House	St. George's Parish	Harford	138
St. Thomas' Church	Garrison Forest	Baltimore County	139
St. Paul's Church		Baltimore City	140
St. John's Church	Kingsville	Baltimore County	141
St. George's Church	Perryman	Harford	142
Christ Church	Easton	Talbot	143
Old Wye Church	Wye Mills	Talbot	144
St. Paul's Church	Centerville	Queen Anne's	145

ILLUSTRATIONS—Concluded

Church		County	Page
Ruins of Whitemarsh	Hambleton	Talbot	146
Christ Church	St. Michael's	Talbot	147
St. Andrew's Church	Princess Anne	Somerset	148
St. Martin's Church	near Berlin	Worcester	149
All Saints' Church	Monii	Somerset	150
Ruins of Coventry Ch.	Rehoboth	Somerset	151
Stepney Church	Green Hill	Wicomico	152
All Hallows Church	Snow Hill	Worcester	153
Site of St. Paul's	Vienna	Dorchester	154
Christ Church	Cambridge	Dorchester	156
Trinity Church	Church Creek	Dorchester	157
Trinity Church	Elkton	Cecil	158
St. Mary's Church	Northeast	Cecil	159
Shrewsbury Church	Locust Grove	Kent	160
St. Stephen's Church	Earleville	Cecil	161
St. Barnabas' Church	Leeland	Prince George's	163
St. Luke's Church	Church Hill	Queen Anne's	164

PREFACE

This book is the embodiment of a desire to make available for reference the data concerning the Establishment of the Church of England in the Province of Maryland, which was authorized by an Act of the Provincial Assembly in 1692. Where possible, information has been added concerning the formation of the parishes with their original metes and bounds, the first Churches built, the first ministers who preached in Maryland and the first vestrymen who served the Church of England in the thirty parishes which were then laid out.

The encouragement given the author by the present Bishop of the Diocese of Maryland, the Rt. Rev. John Gardner Murray, D. D., is gratefully acknowledged. The valuable advice of Mr. Lawrence C. Wroth, Historiographer of the Diocese of Maryland, now Librarian of the John Carter Brown Library, Providence, R. I., the Rev. James M. Magruder and the Rev. Dr. Frank M. Gibson made the work of compiling this book easier and is deeply appreciated.

It was only through the enterprise of The Norman, Remington Company that the publication of this book was made possible. It is the author's hope that this fresh evidence of their interest in Maryland historical writings will meet with the appreciation it deserves from the book buying public. The author deeply appreciates the generosity with which they have treated him at every stage of the book's progress.

To Mr. Albert B. Hoen for the valuable advice and assistance given the author in making the map of Maryland (which accompanies this book) his sincere thanks are extended.

PERCY G. SKIRVEN

Baltimore, Maryland
May 24th, 1923

PART I.
HISTORICAL NOTES

HISTORICAL NOTES

The Protestant Reformation in England resulted in the entrenchment of the Church of England as part of the government of the Kingdom and the consequent displacement of the Roman Catholic Church and the political and social disability of its members. At a later period the Puritan Churches also found themselves under distasteful restrictions and numbers of their adherents began to seek asylum from what they deemed unjust persecution. Coincident with the conception of America as the land of material opportunity had grown the idea of it as a place of refuge, and we find almost from the beginning of the American settlement the two motives animating the successive colonies. The first of these, however, was without religious motive. Virginia had been settled as a commercial venture. New England had meant opportunity and refuge to the Puritans, while the Province of Maryland meant opportunity and refuge to the Roman Catholic colonists whom Lord Baltimore led to the shores of the Chesapeake.

Virginia, settled in 1607, was a stronghold of the Church of England, and Maryland, being a provincial grant to a Roman Catholic, was received by the Roman Catholic Church as an opportunity for initial establishment of its power in this part of the New World. No such event took place, however, for it was not possible to establish an exclusively Roman Catholic colony under the English rule at that time. To this fact may be assigned the primary cause for the "Religious Liberty" enjoyed for nearly half a century by the settlers in the Province of Maryland.

2   THE FIRST PARISHES OF THE PROVINCE OF MARYLAND

Prior to the landing of Lord Baltimore's colonists at St. Mary's there were no settlements within the limits of the Province as specified in the Charter with the exception of those on the "Isle of Kent" and on Palmer's Island. The latter was within the mouth of the Susquehanna river. Eight years prior to the landing of the colonists, whom the fancy of one of Maryland's brilliant historians[1] has led him to call "Pilgrims," William Cleyborne traded, under license, with the Indians in the upper Chesapeake bay, establishing in 1631 a Trading Post on the "Isle of Kent." In that year there were about one hundred souls in that settlement and in 1632 the settlers sent a representative to the Virginia Assembly at Jamestown.[2]

In that year, 1631, Cleyborne brought to the "Isle of Kent" from Hampton, Virginia, the Rev. Richard James who conducted there the first service of the Church of England said to have been held in the territory now lying within the borders of Maryland. As this minister went to Virginia from England, "certified" by the Bishop of London, and thence to the "Isle of Kent," it will be observed that this was the first regular planting of the Church of England on what is now Maryland soil. It is quite probable that Mr. James conducted these services in the small fort which had been built on the extreme southern end of the island as a protection against the Indians.

The poet tells us that the "Pilgrims" of New England went to that land seeking "Freedom to worship God," but it was to the Province of Maryland, first of all the American colonies, that all creeds went assured of their freedom to worship as their conscience dictated. McMahon says "Religious liberty was subject only to the restraints of Conscience."[3] Very naturally the question arises how such a

---
[1] McMahon, History of Maryland, p. 198.
[2] Chalmer's Political Annals of United Colonies, p. 206, also Henning's Statutes at Large, Vol. 1, p. 154.
[3] McMahon, History of Maryland, p. 198.

condition was brought about since George Calvert, the first Lord Baltimore, was an avowed Roman Catholic and Cecilius Calvert, his son, who succeeded to his father's titles and estates, becoming the second Lord Baltimore, was also a Roman Catholic.

Born of Church of England parents at Kipling, Yorkshire, England, in 1582, George Calvert early developed into a man of large capabilities. James I, recognizing in him the qualities of an excellent business man as well as an astute politician, made Calvert one of his Secretaries of State in 1619.[1] In frankly announcing his conversion to the Roman Catholic Church he so impressed the King with his honesty that he was continued in the Privy Council and later, in 1625, made Baron Baltimore of Baltimore, in the County of Longford, Ireland.

Having failed in a former endeavor toward colonizing in bleak Newfoundland[2] George Calvert made a voyage, in 1629, to the Southern mainland of North America. Being impressed with what he saw, during this visit, in the Virginia Colony he asked for the territory now known as Maryland. There he had expected to offset the loss of the money sunk in his ill-fated project at Avalon and to build a fortune for himself and his family. There was also another object that he had in mind. As a secondary consideration he wanted to establish a refuge for his Roman Catholic friends—a place where they could practice their religious ceremonies without interference. Destined never to realize his cherished ambitions George Calvert died in April, 1632, before his promised charter to Maryland received the Great Seal.

The death of George Calvert did not prevent King Charles from signing the Charter on June 20, 1632, grant-

---

[1] Ency. Brit., 9th Edit., Vol. IV, p. 713.
[2] The Charter to Avalon, Newfoundland, was a gift from King James in further recognition of George Calvert's faithful services.

ing to Cecilius Calvert, the second Lord Baltimore, all that his father had asked. In giving him the Province of Maryland Charles I placed Cecilius Calvert in absolute ownership of all the land[1] lying within the bounds of the Province. McMahon says "this Charter was the most ample and sovereign that ever emanated from the English Crown."[2] In the Charter appears the following: "And We do by these Presents . . . make, create and constitute Him, the now Baron of Baltimore, and his heirs, the true and absolute Lords and Proprietaries of the Region [Maryland] aforesaid . . ."[3] There would seem to be nothing to prevent Cecilius Calvert from using his authority, thus conferred, to adopt any religious policy for his Province that his ambitions dictated. True there was a provision in the Charter which held in check any very radical change from the laws of the mother country. The provision read in part: "So nevertheless, that *all* Laws aforesaid be Consonant to Reason and be not repugnant or contrary, but (so far as convenient may be) *agreeable* to the *Laws, Statutes, Customs* and *Rights* of this *Our Kingdom* of *England* . . ."[4]

In recognition of the magnificent gift, the Province of Maryland, and in acknowledgment of the overlordship of the King, Cecilius Calvert was required to yield "therefore unto US, our Heirs and Successors, two Indian Arrows of those parts, to be delivered at the said Castle of Windsor, every year on Tuesday in Easter-week: and also the fifth part of all Gold and Silver Ore, which shall happen from time to time, to be found within the aforesaid Limits."[5]

[1] McMahon, History of Maryland, p. 167.
[2] McMahon, History of Maryland, p. 155.
[3] Charter, Section V.
[4] Charter, Section VII.
[5] Charter, Section V.

The second Lord Baltimore, Cecilius Calvert, was a great-hearted far-sighted nobleman endowed with good common sense. He realized that he possessed an exceedingly valuable gift in this fine domain, interlaced as it was with beautiful rivers and divided by the great Chesapeake Bay. He appreciated fully the meaning of the various provisions of his Charter. He also realized that he held this Charter under a Protestant government and owing to the existing religious feeling in England it was impossible, "Absolute Lord" though he was, to establish an exclusively Roman Catholic colony. He shrewdly adopted as his policy "Religious liberty," for by doing so he avoided all conditions that tended to mar the success of his undertaking[1] of colonizing Maryland. He made no misstep, nor did he miscalculate his plans, for he was in possession of all the knowledge we now have bearing on those times, and also had the advantage of breathing the atmosphere of English politics of the day. Second only to the territory itself Calvert's policy of "Religious liberty" was his most valuable *asset*. Like all good business men he looked after his business assets with great care.

The encouragement given Cecilius Calvert by the gift of so generous a "grant" was sufficient to induce him to make a great outlay of money to fit out two vessels, the "Ark" and the "Dove," and also to provide nearly 300 colonists for the voyage to the Province in North America. The expedition left England on Saint Cecilia's Day, November 22nd, 1633, and Leonard Calvert, a brother of the Proprietary, was sent out as governor of the Province. After a long and stormy voyage by way of the West Indies they came into the Chesapeake on the 27th of February,

---

[1] "The system of toleration was co-eval with the colony itself; and sprang from the liberal and *sagacious* views of the first proprietary." McMahon's Hist. of Maryland, p. 226.

1634. After sailing about the bay looking for the best place to found the city which they intended to build in the Province, they decided to land on an island in the Potomac River which they named "St. Clements." Having made the selection of that place, they waited a day or two, probably in order that they might land on Lady's Day, the Feast of the Annunciation, March 25th, 1634. Upon going ashore they erected a cross and took possession "In the name of the Savior of the World and of the King of England." This was nearly three years after the Rev. Richard James, Priest of the Church of England, first ministered on the Isle of Kent.

The numerical majority of those who came to the Province in the "Ark" and the "Dove" were of the Anglican Faith.[1] The principal adventurers were Roman Catholics and as a consequence the religious tone of the early province was Roman Catholic.

There does not appear to be any record of an Anglican Clergyman among them nor of services held according to the rites of the Church of England very soon after the landing of the colonists. It is generally believed that Anglicans and Roman Catholics for some years used the same chapel at St. Mary's for worship. Doubtless the Anglican Church services were read by lay readers or by visiting clergymen from the neighboring colony of Virginia.[2]

Under the date of the 13th of November, 1633, Cecilius Calvert had given instructions to Governor Leonard Calvert and his two Commissioners, before they sailed from England for the Province, as follows:—

---

[1] Johnson's Founders of Maryland, p. 22.
[2] The Rev. William Wilkinson, Rector of St. George's Church, Poplar Hill, 1650-1663, had loaned money in this vicinity previous to his moving from Virginia to Maryland as a permanent resident and apparently was drawn thither in person by the opportunity of ministering to the adherents of the Established Church of England.

VIEW OF ST. MARY'S RIVER AT ST. MARY'S CITY

Here Gov. Leonard Calvert landed, in 1634, and here the foundation of Religious Liberty in America eventually was established.

"No. 1 Impri. His lordship requires his said Governor and Commissioners that in their voyage to Maryland they be very careful to preserve unity and peace amongst all passengers on Shipboard, and that they suffer no scandal nor offence to be given to any of the Protestants whereby any just complaint may hereafter be made by them in Virginia or in England. And that for that end they cause all Acts of Roman Catholique Religion to be done as privately as may be, and that they instruct all the Roman Catholiques to be silent upon all occasions of discourse concerning matters of Religion, and that the said Governor and Commissioners treate the Protestants with as much mildness and favor as Justice will permit. And this to be observed at Land as well as at Sea."[1]

It is apparent that Cecilius Calvert realized that it was essential that no offence be given to the Protestants. And also that only the fairest treatment of the colonists upon their arrival in the newly discovered country would keep the Province in his hands.

Indeed Calvert intended from the moment he conceived the idea of founding the Province of Maryland to insure religious toleration in the province by writing into his instructions orders to that effect. It is evident that he carried out his intention. As a case in point to show how diligently Leonard Calvert, governor of the province, carried out the wishes of his brother, that of William Lewis, the steward of Thomas Cornwallis, a Roman Catholic, can profitably be told here. Losing control of himself when two of his fellow servants read aloud from a volume of Smith's Sermons certain passages reflecting upon the

[1] Narratives of Early Maryland (C. C. Hall), p. 16.

Pope and the Roman Catholic faith, Lewis made the assertion, it was alleged, that all Protestant ministers were "ministers of the devil." Governor Calvert with a Roman Catholic Court immediately fined him 500 pounds of tobacco and exacted a bond from him for good behavior lest he should "again offend the peace of the colony . . . by injudicious and unnecessary argument or disputation in matters of religion; . . . or use any ignominious words or speeches touching the books or ministers authorized by the State of England."[1]

Following up these instructions to his brother Leonard, Cecilius Calvert issued in 1636 instructions for his future governors and also an oath of office which included the following:

> "I will not by myself, or any other, directly or indirectly trouble, molest or discountenance any person professing to believe in Jesus Christ for or in respect of religion. I will make no difference of persons in conferring offices, favors or rewards for or in respect of religion, but merely as they shall be found faithful and well deserving and endued with moral virtue and abilities. My aim shall be public unity and that if any person or official shall molest any person professing to believe in Jesus Christ on account of his religion I will protect the person molested and punish the offender."[2]

This oath was the forerunner of the so-called "Toleration Act" passed by the Assembly twelve years later. Shortly after promulgation of the Governor's oath, the first building was erected, in 1642 for the Church of England

---

[1] Arch. Md. Prov. Council, 1637–1650, p. 35.
[2] McMahon's History of Maryland, p. 226. (Chalmers says "this oath was taken by the Governors and Council from 1637 to 1657," see Political Annals.)

worshippers in St. Mary's County—Trinity Church.[1] Without the formal induction of a minister, the congregation worshipped there without interference. Further up the Potomac River and some three or four miles across the St. Mary's, Poplar Hill (St. George's) Church was built about the same time. It was in this Church in 1650 that the first permanently settled Church of England clergyman, the Rev. William Wilkinson, began his thirteen years of ministry. Another church was built for the Protestants at St. Clement's Manor, about the same time as Trinity and Poplar Hill were. This church was built by Thomas Gerrard "for the convenience" of his Protestant wife, her friends and servants. In the building of these churches may be perceived the immediate results of Lord Baltimore's assurances of protection to the colonists in religious worship. Up to this time no other parts of the colony had attempted the building of a church. While it is true that no churches were built, it is known that there had been places of worship, however primitive they may have been, on Kent Island and in Kent County on the north side of Chester River about the year 1652. As proof of there being no Protestant minister in the colony at that time, a fine of five hundred pounds of tobacco upon a colonist was to be paid to the first Protestant minister "to arrive" in the colony.[2]

When Charles I[3] was deposed, and opposition to the King which culminated later in the establishment of the Commonwealth under Cromwell developed, Lord Baltimore set about to solve the difficult problem of retaining pos-

[1] Trinity Church, at St. Mary's City, now stands on the site. There were no churches built for Roman Catholic worship in the Province because of that part of the Charter, Section IV, which expressly says: "The Patronages and advowsons of all churches which within the said Region . . . shall happen to be built . . . the same to be dedicated and consecrated according to the Ecclesiastical Laws of our Kingdom of England."
[2] Arch. Md. Prov. Council, 1637-1650, p. 35.
[3] Charles I was beheaded 30th January, 1649, Ency. Brit., 9th Edition.

session of his colony. With characteristic shrewdness he concluded that the best way to do this was to change the "complexion" of the Council so that it would give to the Protestants a majority. Prior to this change (1648) the Assembly, it is said, had been composed almost entirely of Roman Catholic members. With this exhibition of willingness to satisfy the Protestants, he went further and appointed a Protestant Governor of the colony, William Stone. Feeling that his province was still in danger of confiscation, he urged in 1649 the passage by the Assembly of the "Act Concerning Religion"[1] which became known as the "Maryland Toleration Act." The preamble to the act is as follows:

> "For as much as in a well governed Xtian Common Wealth matters concerning Religion and the honor of God ought in the first place to be taken into serious consideration and endeavored to be settled. Be it therefore ordered and enacted by the R^t Honble Cecilius Lord Baron of Baltimore Absolute Lord and Proprietary of this Province, with the advice and consent of this General Assembly. . . ."

The first clause in the "Act" was as follows:

> "That whatsoever person or persons within the Province and the Islands thereunto belonging shall from henceforth blaspheme God, that is Curse him or deny our Saviour Jesus Christ to bee the sonne of God, or shall deny the Holy Trinity the Father, sonne and holy Ghost, or the Godhead of any of the s^d Three Persons or the Trinity or the Unity of the Godhead or shall use or utter any reproachful Speeches, words or languages concerning the said Holy Trinity or any of the said Three persons

[1] Arch. Md., Vol. I, p. 244.

thereof, shall be punished with death and confiscation or forfeiture of all his or her lands and goods to the Lord Proprietary and his heires."

The law further provided against the calling of names. The enumeration of these is interesting because the list apparently includes the names of some of the sects then within the Province—they are "Heretick, Scismatick, Idolator, Puritan, Independent, Prespiterian, Popish Priest, Jesuit, Jesuited Papist, Lutheran, Calvinist, Anabaptist, Brownist, Antinomian, Barrowist, Roundhead and Separatist." The Sabbath was not to be profaned. The last clause and most important of all was as follows:

"That no person or persons whatsoever within this Province, . . . , professing to believe in Jesus Christ, shall from henceforth bee any waies troubled, Molested or discountenanced for or in respect of his or her religion nor in the free exercise thereof within this Province or Islands thereunto belonging nor any way compelled to the beliefe or exercise of any other Religion against his or her consent, soe as they be not unfaithful to the Lord Proprietary, or molest or conspire against the civil Government established, or to be established, in this Province under him or his heires."[1]

The passage of the "Toleration Act" was published in England and had its effect on the migration to the Province. Men of character and wealth were attracted to this delightful country of the New World. The numerous religious sects, finding full protection there in their religious worship, lived in harmony with their neighbors. Maryland, first of all the American colonies, had completed all the conditions that afforded to the World what it had for centuries longed for—

[1] Arch. Md., Vol. I, p. 246.

Religious Liberty. By persistently adhering to his original plan Cecilius Calvert had the satisfaction of realizing that his foresight was good in avoiding any condition that would compromise his ownership of the Province. How well he and his successors governed the Province nearly a half century is told by McMahon.[1] "Conspicuous above every other colony of that period, for its uniform regard of religious liberty, it had its reward. Harmony, peace and prosperity, were the general results; and this period in the history of Maryland, may be truly styled 'the golden age of its colonial existence.'"

From the beginning of the Province up to the Protestant Revolution in 1689 the missionary work of the Church of England was productive of very little result. The Church was interested in the missionary work in Virginia[2] but the work in Maryland was hampered by the provisions of Calvert's Charter. Cooperation between the Proprietary and the Church was practically impossible. Baltimore neglected to appoint ministers of the Church to "livings" in the Province. An effort was made in 1661 in the Lower House of the Provincial Assembly to provide a "maynetenance for ministers," but two days later, May 1st, 1661, upon the reading of the bill in the Upper House, "It was voted to be altogether insufficient and short of the thing aimed at."[3] However this did not prevent the gradual growth of the Church and throughout the Province the faithful Churchmen held the regular services.

On Kent Island a church was built on Broad Creek about the year 1652. This was near where the Rev. Richard

---

[1] McMahon History of Maryland, p. 228.
[2] "In 1629 the Bishop of London announced the jurisdiction of the Church of England over the religious affairs of the Virginia colony on the James River. That was the beginning of the official missionary movement in America," see Hawks, Vol. 1, p. 38.
[3] Arch. Md., Vol. I, p. 406.

James had preached eighteen years earlier. Upon the death of the Rev. William Wilkinson in 1663, the Rev. Francis Sourton became rector of old Poplar Hill Church in St. Mary's County. At a church in Baltimore County on Bush River the Rev. John Yeo preached in 1683. In Calvert County the Rev. William Mullett held services in 1684. In 1682 in Anne Arundel County the Rev. Duell Pead baptized children. The Assembly at St. Mary's asked this same minister, in October, 1683 to preach to both the Upper and Lower Houses on October 14th, 1683, which he did and this interesting record of the proceedings of the Assembly of the 20th of October, 1683, gives an insight into the religious conditions that obtained at that time in the province. It is as follows:

"Upper House 20th October, 1683.

This house having taken into their serious consideration the great Care and Kindness of Our Sovereign Lord the King in giving in charge to the Right Reverend Father in God the Bishop of London to Supply this Place with able and Devout Ministers whereby the people may know their Duty to God and their Obedience to their Rulers do request the Lower House of this Assembly to Join with this House in giving thanks to M[r] Duell Pead for his Learned Sermon preached before these two Houses the 14th Instant and that some Acceptable Present be given him for the same and this House is willing to concur with them therein.

Signed pr. Order Thos. Gounwin,
Clerk of Assembly."

The Lower House concurred on the 24th of October, 1683, and gave him a vote of thanks, only. The ministers whom we have just mentioned were among the earliest of the clergy to come to the province to engage in missionary work.

14 THE FIRST PARISHES OF THE PROVINCE OF MARYLAND

Before William of Orange ascended the throne, Lord Baltimore is said to have opposed the revolution in England[1] which conferred the crown on William. The enemies, in England, of Lord Baltimore induced the King to uphold the "rebellious" body of men in Maryland who had overthrown in 1689 the Proprietary's officials there. The work of the "associators" popularly described as the "Protestant Revolution" (1689) has been overfeatured as a factor in influencing the King to terminate the rule of the Calverts. It was a factor, but viewed from Whitehall, it was regarded more as an excuse than as a cause. The die had been cast.

On the 21st of August, 1690, proceedings were instituted at Whitehall, London, against the Charter of the Calverts in order to "vacate"[2] it and an address to the Colonists under date of the 12th of March, 1691, was sent to Maryland in which appears the following:

". . . Wee have thought fitt to take our Province of Maryland under our immediate care and Protection and by letters Patents under the Great Seal of England to appoint our Trusty and well beloved Lionel Copley, Esq., of whose prudence and loyalty we are assured, to be our Governor thereof."[3]

This ended the rule of the Calverts as Roman Catholics, and not until 1715, after the accession of King George I, were the powers of government restored to them. The then Proprietary, Charles Calvert, infant son of Benedict Calvert, Lord Baltimore, had been educated in "the established religion of England and had thus become capable of holding governmental authorities subordinate to the Crown."[4] He

[1] F. L. Hawks, Vol. 2, p. 57, "Ecclesiastical History of the United States."
[2] Arch. Md., Vol. 8, p. 200.
[3] Arch. Md., Vol. 8, p. 235.
[4] Kilty's "Landowner's Assistant," p. 163.

OLD OAK TREE

St. Paul's Cemetery, Kent County

Undoubtedly standing at the time of the Establishment, 1692. It is one of several mammoth oaks that shade this beautiful spot. The circumference of the trunk of this tree, one foot above the ground, is 32 feet. The greatest spread of branches is 128 feet.

governed the province under the guidance of his guardian, Lord Guilford.

This also was the end of "Religious Liberty" which had been the principal "asset" of the Calverts and to which particular attention has been called.[1] "Religious Liberty," the child of expediency, was supplanted by no weakling when the king extended the jurisdiction of the Church of England to the Province of Maryland. Governor Copley's commission, dated February 14th, 1691, outlined the policy he was to pursue. The establishing of the Church of England by law was one of the first movements he was to set on foot. The right of induction of ministers was vested in him and upon close examination of his instructions it will be seen that he came to Maryland as the personal representative of both the Crown and the Church of England. Notice what this part of his instructions says:

". . . and you are to enquire whether there be any minister within your Government who Preaches and Administers the Sacrament in any orthodox Church or Chappell without being in due Orders whereof you are to give an account to the said Bishop of London."[2]

At the meeting of the first Assembly, May, 1692, at the City of St. Mary's, after Governor Copley came, the first act passed was for the repealing of all previous laws. This done, the Assembly was presented with the draft of the Act entitled "An Act for the Service of Almighty God and the Establishment of the Protestant Religion within this Province." The provisions of this Act had been thoroughly discussed during the session, the first mention of the Act being found in the proceedings of May 16th, 1692. On June 2nd the House and Council both assented to the bill

---
[1] See also Act of 1702, p. 71, this book.
[2] Arch. Md., Vol. 8, p. 276.

and on June 9th, Governor Copley invited all the members of both houses to witness his signature to this Act. The first provision of the Act read as follows:

> "Be it therefore enacted by the King and Queens most Excellent Majestys by and with the advice and consent of this present General Assembly and the authority of the same That the Church of England within this Province shall have and enjoy all her Rights Liberties and Franchises wholly inviolable as is now or shall be hereafter Established by Law and also that the Great Charter of England be kept and observed in all points."[1]

Under the authority of this Act, the justices of each of the ten counties of Maryland were instructed to meet at their respective Court Houses, having previously given notice to the freeholders also to attend the meeting. With the advice of the freeholders the counties were to be divided into parishes. The vestrymen elected for each parish were to be of the freeholders, six in number, and the orthodox minister to be one of the vestry in his respective parish. Churches were to be built in each parish and a tax of forty pounds of tobacco was to be laid on the people of the province irrespective of creed for the maintenance of the minister. The provisions of this Act were carried out and the work of dividing the counties into parishes was completed in the following year, full reports of the work in each county being made to the Governor and Council by the County Clerks.

The "instructions" to Governor Copley, given him upon leaving England, included a command to

> ". . . take especial care that God Almighty be devoutly and duly served within your Govern-

[1] Arch. Md., Vol. 13, p. 425.

ment; the book of Common Prayer as it is now established read each Sunday and Holiday and the Blessed Sacrament administered according to the Rites of the Church of England. You shall take care that the churches already built there shall be well and orderly kept and more built as the Colony by God's Blessing be improved and that besides a competent maintenance be assigned to the minister of each church, a convenient house built at the common charge for each minister. You are not to prefer any minister to any Ecclesiastical Benefice in that Our Province without a certificate from the Right Reverend the Bishop of London of his being conformable to the doctrine and discipline of the Church of England and of a good life and conversation."[1]

The reports to the Assembly in 1694 made by the Justices of the ten different counties of the Province showed that there were then thirty parishes, twenty-two churches and nine ministers.

Upon the death of Governor Copley,[2] Sir Francis Nicholson was sent out as Governor of the Province,[3] and to him the work of building up the Church was a pleasure. He wrote to the Board of Trade and Plantation in March, 1697, as follows:—

"There was a law passed in the late Governor Copley's time for establishing the Church of England which his Majesty in Council was pleased to disapprove and disallow of &c; But there is another law now sent to your Lordships, and you may please to see by the Journals of the Assembly, what difficulties I met with about it. When I came

[1] Arch. Md., Vol. 8, p. 276.
[2] September 9th, 1693.
[3] Gov. Nicholson arrived in the province in July, 1694.

hither I found very few of the Churches built, but I hope in God that they will be all finished this year, and then we shall want Clergymen, and a Commissary to inspect the Church affairs, for whose maintenance an Act is passed, and now sent to your Lordships. My Lord Bishop of London hath promised to send an able Commissary and some good Clergymen."[1]

Governor Nicholson took the greatest interest in perfecting the Establishment and offered by way of an incentive "that if a way can be found out to build a house in every parish for the ministers, his Excellency (Nicholson) does propose to give five pounds sterling towards building every such house begun in his Excellency's time." His influence was the strongest help the Church of England had in Maryland at that time. The expenses of transportation of the ministers into the province was allowed them and in the year 1697, nine more clergymen came into the colony, making in all eighteen.[2]

The time had now arrived for a personal representative of the Bishop of London to take charge of the affairs of the Church. Dr. Thomas Bray was one of the greatest of the missionaries ever sent out from England and was noted for his godliness and great intelligence. Born 1656 at Marton, Shropshire, he was educated at Oxford. After serving as rector of Sheldon for a number of years (during these years he was devoting much of his time to collecting libraries for the use of the missionaries), he was sent to Maryland by Bishop Compton, then Lord Bishop of London, to settle the affairs of the infant Church.[3] Doctor Bray left England on December 20th, 1699, and arrived

[1] Arch. Md., Vol. 23, p. 82.
[2] See Section VII for list of Churches and Clergy in 1696.
[3] Encyclo. Brit., "Dr. Bray."

THE FIRST PARISHES OF THE PROVINCE OF MARYLAND

in Maryland in March following. Going at once to Annapolis, he summoned the clergy to a "visitation," which was held in that city on May 23rd, 1700. There were present seventeen clergymen representing fifteen of the parishes. To these he delivered a charge and gave them instructions in their clerical work. This good man was able so to impress the importance of the Establishment upon both the clergy and the Assembly that the work received a great impetus.

After a short period (less than six months) of hard work in the Province in the interest of the Church, Doctor Bray returned to England to help in getting a law passed that would firmly establish the Church in Maryland. Those laws for the Establishment which the Assembly passed in 1692, 1696 and 1700 had defects which caused their "disallowance" by the King when they were presented in council at Whitehall. Doctor Bray, having had the intimate knowledge of the conditions in the Province as well as of the requirements necessary to have the law passed at the King's Council, advised the Assembly at Annapolis first to have the law framed by the Commissioners of Trade and Plantation in England and then to pass it as it came from them. Doctor Bray gave his personal attention to the law, and when the Assembly convened at Annapolis in March, 1702, Governor Nathaniel Blackistone instructed the members of the Assembly to "fill in the blanks and pass the bill without amendment." This was done! The Assembly adjourned on the 25th of March, 1702, having passed the "Act for the Establishment of Religious worship in this Province According to the Church of England and for the Maintainance of Ministers." By that act the Church in Maryland was governed, for over seventy years—until the outbreak of the Revolutionary War in 1775.

PART II.

PAPERS RELATING TO THE RELIGIOUS CONDITIONS THAT OBTAINED IN THE PROVINCE PRIOR TO THE ESTABLISHMENT.

Queries from Whitehall and Answers by Lord Baltimore, Address to King William, Instructions to Governor Copley, Names of Associators, 1690, Members of Council and Assembly, 1692, Changes in Personnel, Laws Repealed, 1692, etc., etc.

QUERIES ABOUT MARYLAND PROPOUNDED BY THE COMMISSIONERS OF TRADE AND PLANTATION.

"At the Committee of Trade and Plantations, Monday the 10th of Aprill 1676 at the Robes Chamber in Whitehall.

Present

Lord Privy Seale	Earle of Craven
Duke of Ormond	Mr Sec^{ty} Williamson
Earle of Carlisle	

There was also prepared the draft of a letter to the Lords Proprietors of Carolina, the Lord Baltimore Proprietor of Maryland, Sir George Carteret Proprietor of New Jersey, and to the Bermudas Company, setting forth how that the plantation business (managed lately by a particular Councill) was now referred by his Majesty to a Committee of his Privy Councill, and that their Lordships might be enabled to inform his Majesty touching the condition of those Colonies. Their Lordships do send them some heads of Enquiry, upon which they are to return an accompt."[1]

"Their Lordships on the 10th of April sign a Circular letter wth severall Heads of Inquiry to the Lord Baltimore Lord Proprietary of Maryland.[2]

The letter followeth.

After our very hearty commendacōns to your Lordship. His Majesty having in his wisdom thought fit to supersede the Commission by which his Council of Trade & Forreign Plantations lately acted & thereby restoring all the business of

[1] Arch. Md., Vol. 5, p. 125.
[2] Arch. Md., Vol. 5, p. 128.

that nature to its accustomed Chanel of a Committee of his Privy Council. And his maj^ty having more especially committed to a select number of the Board, whereof we are, the care and management of things relating to his Plantations, we have therefore thought it convenient to give your Lord^sp advirtism^t thereof. And because we do not as yet find ourselves enabled to give his Matie such account of the State & Condition of that Colony as his Royall service & the dependence thereof upon the Crown does require. We have therefore thought fit to send your Ld^p (as we have done to others) some Heads of Inquiry here añext, the better to guide your Lordship in the method of that state and representation of things which we expect from your Lordship, and do desire it may be done with all convenient speed.

And soe not doubting of your Lordships care to advise us farther in all matters that may from time to time conduce to his ma^ties service, & our better discharge of the trust reposed in us.

We bid your Lordship very hearty farewell."

The questions most important to the subject are:

"From the Council Chamber at Whitehall[1]
This Tenth of April 1676"

No. 11. *Trade Building.* What are the principal Towns and Places of trade. And what manner of Buildings are most used in your Colony as to the strength and largeness of them.

No. 12. *Parishes.* How many Parishes, Precincts or Divisions are within your Lordship's Province?

[1] Arch. Md., Vol. 5, p. 128.

No. 18. *Christenings.* What number of Whites, Blacks or Mulattos have been born and Christened for these seven years last past, or any other space of time for as many years as you are able to state an account of?

No. 19. *Marriages.* What number of Mariages for seaven years last past or any other time, for as many years as you are able to state an account of?

No. 20. *Burials.* What number of people have yearly dyed within your Province for seaven years past or any other time, for as many years as you are able to state an account of?

No. 26. *Religion.* What persuasion in Religious matters is most prevalent; and among the varieties which you are to express which proportion in members and quality of people the one holds to the other.

No. 27. *Church:* What course is taken for the instructing of the people in the Christian Religion? How many Churches and Ministers are there within your Province and how many are yet wanting for the accommodation of your Colony? What provision is there made for their maintenance as also for relieving the poor decayed and impotent persons? And whether you have any Beggars or idle Vagabonds?"

RELIGIOUS CONDITIONS IN THE PROVINCE OF MARYLAND 1676

Writing from the Patuxent river section of the Province under date of 25th May 1676, the Rev. John Yeo, a Church of England clergyman, labouring as a missionary in Maryland at that time, calls thea ttention of the Archbishop of Canterbury to the religious situation which confronted him. His letter is in part as follows:

"Most Reverend Father:

> Please to Pardon this Presumption of Mine in presenting to your serious view these Rude & indigested lines w^{ch} (with humble submission) are to acquaint yor Grace with the Deplorable estate & condition of the Province of Maryland for want of an established Ministry, here are in this Province tenn or twelve County's & in them at least twenty thousand soules & but *three* Protestant ministers of us th^t are Conformable to the Doctrine & Discipline of the Church of England."

He writes of those who pretend they are ministers and states that they are not qualified and

> "for the most part such as never understood anything of learning & yet take upon themselves to be Dispensers of the Word & to administer Sacrament of Baptisme & sow seeds of Divission amongst the People & noe law Provided for the Suppression of such in this Province soe th^t here is a great necessitie of able & learned men to confute the gaine sayer especially having so many Profest enemies as the Popish Priests & Jesuits are, who are encouraged & Provided for & the Quaker takes care & provides for those that are Speakers in their Con-

venticles, but noe care is taken or Provision made for the building up Christians in the Protestant Religion by means whereof not only many Dayly fall away either to Popery, Quakerism or Phanaticisme but also the Lord's Day is prophaned, Religion dispised, & all notorious vices committed soe th^t it is become a Sodom of uncleaness and a Pest house of iniquity.

I doubt not but yor Grace will take it into Consideration & do yor utmost for our Eternall welfaire, & now is the time th^t yor Grace may be an instrument of a universal reformation amongst us with greatest facillity. Cacillius Lord Barron Baltimore & Absolute Proprietor of Maryland being dead and Charles Lord Barron of Baltimore & our governor being bound for England this year (as I am Informed) to Receive a farther confirmation of that Province from his Majestie at wh^{ch} time I doubt but yor Grace may soe prevaile with him as th^t a maintenance for a Protestant ministry may be established as well in this Province as in Virginia, Barbadoes and all other his Majesties Plantations etc., etc.

Yo^r Most Obedient Son & Servt
John Yeo.

To
The Most Reverend Father in God
Gilbert by Divine Providence
Lord Archbishop of Canterbury
            and
   Metropolitan of England
   at his Palace at Lambith."[1]

[1] Arch. Md., Vol. 5, p. 130.

The letter was received in due course by the Arch-Bishop and being convinced of the earnestness of the appeal wrote to the Bishop of London as follows:

"Croydon,[1]
August 2nd 1676.

My Lord:

The enclosed came lately unto me, and from a person altogether unknown. The design there in proposed, seem's very honest and is in itself so laudable that I conceive it concerns us by all means to promote it:

If your Lordship shall please to remember it, when the Lord Baltimores affaires comes to be considered of at the Councel Table, I make no question but there may be a convenient opportunity to obtain some settled revenue for the ministry of that place as well as the other plantations; when that is once done, it will be no difficult matter for us to supply them with such as are of competent abilities to undertake the employment and with all such as we know to be both regular and conformable.

I bid your Lordship heartily farewel and am My Lord your Lordships

Most affect: Friend and Brother
Gilb: Cant:"

No action was taken upon the matter until the meeting of the Lords of Trade and Plantation on July 19, 1677[2] at which meeting Lord Baltimore appeared before the Board in person. The minutes of that meeting state—"On reading a letter from the Archbishop of Canterbury to the Bishop of London, Lord Baltimore presented a paper[3] setting forth the present religion in Maryland."

[1] Arch. Md., Vol. 5, p. 132.
[2] Calendar of State Papers, America and West Indies, Vol. 1677-1678, p.121.
[3] See Lord Baltimore's Paper on next page.

"WHEREUPON THE LORD BALTIMORE PRESENTS A PAPER SETTING FORTH THE PRESENT STATE OF RELIGION IN MARYLAND, VIZ^T

That for the encouragement of all such persons as were desirous and willing to adventure and transport themselves & families into the Province of Maryland a law there made by the advice and consent of the Delegates of the Freemen concerning Religion, wherein a toleration is given to all persons believing in Jesus Christ freely to exercise their Religion & that no person of what judgement soever, believing as aforesaid should at any time be molested or discountenanced for or in respect of his Religion or in the free exercise thereof and that noe one should be compelled to the beliefe or exercise of any other [Religion] against his consent. Upon this Act the greatest part of the people and Inhabitants now in Maryland have setled themselves & families there & for these many years this toleration & liberty has been known & continued in the Government of that Province.

That those persons of the Church of England there who at any time have encouraged any ministers to come over into that Province have had several sent unto them as at this time there are residing there foure that the Ld Baltimore knows of who have Plantations & settled beings of their owne and those that have not any such beings are maintained by a voluntary contribution of those of their own persuasion, as others of the Presbiterians, Independents, Anabaptists, Quakers & Romish Church are.

That in every Country [county?] in the Province of Maryland there are a sufficient number of Churches and

[1] Arch. Md., Vol. V. p. 133, July 19, 1677.

Houses called Meeting Houses for the people there and these have been built and are still kept in good repaire by a free and voluntary contribution of all such as frequent the said Churches and Meeting Houses. That the Laws of that Province have been ever made by the advice and consent of the Freemen by their Delegates assembled as well as by the Proprietor and his Council and without the consent of all these no law there has been made.

That the Laws of that Province have been ever made by the advice and consent of the Freemen by their Delegates assembled as well as by the Proprietor and his Councill and without the consent of *all* these no Law there has been made.

The greatest part of the Inhabitants of that Province (three of four at least) doe consist of Presbiterians, Independents, Anabaptists and Quakers, those of the Church of England as well as those of the Romish being the fewest, so that it will be a most difficult task to draw such persons to consent unto a Law, which shall compel them to maintain ministers of a contrary persuasion to themselves, they having already an assurance by that Act for Religion that they have all freedom in point of Religion and Divine Worship and noe penalties or payments imposed upon them in that particular. That in Carolina, New Jersey and Roade Island, the Inhabitants for the peopling of those places have had and still have the same toleration that those in Maryland have."

After the submission of the foregoing paper by Lord Baltimore the minutes of the Lords of Trade and Plantation have the following entry:

"Whereupon their Lordships sign a letter to Lord Baltimore as follows:

Have received very credible information that many inhabitants of Maryland live very dissolute

THE FIRST PARISHES OF THE PROVINCE OF MARYLAND 31

lives, committing notorious vices and prophaning the Lord's Day. Hope there are sufficient Laws to restrain and punish such evil lives and oblige men to live at least *like* Christians, though not of the same profession. If the laws be full enough desire his Lord[sp] to have them put in execution, or, if defective to pass such laws as the occassion requires.

Have reason to believe this wicked kind of living proceed from there being no certain established allowance for ministers of the gospel, especially of the Protestant religion according to the Church of England, the cause of a great want of able ministers. Know how necessary it is to have this want supplied without imposing any burthen upon the inhabitants that they are willing freely to settle, therefore desire his Lord[sp] to write to the Governor and Council of Maryland to send over an account of the number of Protestant ministers of the Church of England and their allowances, also of the number of Protestant families and the value of their Plantations and how many congregations they make up; also to inquire what each congregation will freely settle for the maintenance of an able minister which, when agreed upon, to be enacted into a law as in His Majesty's other Plantations.

Would likewise be glad to have account of the number of ministers or teachers of dissenters and their allowances, and of the number of the planters, their persuasions, and the number of each persuasion."[1]

Lord Baltimore's answers to the "Quiries" which appear on page 24, and to the above letter are set forth in part as follows:

[1] Calendar of State Papers, America and West Indies, Vol. 2. 1677-1678, p. 121

ANSWER OF LORD BALTIMORE TO THE QUERIES ABOUT MARYLAND PROPOUNDED BY COMMISSIONERS OF TRADE AND PLANTATION
26th March 1678

"Answer to No. 11—*Trade Building and* No. 12—*Parishes.* [1]

The people there [Maryland] not affecting to build nere each other but soe as to have their houses nere the water for convenience of trade and their lands on each side of and behind their houses by which it happens that in most places there are not fifty houses in the space of thirty miles. And for this reason it is that they have been hitherto only able to divide the Province into Counties without being able to make any *subdivisions* into Parishes or precincts which is a work not to be effected until it shall please God to increase the number of the people and so to alter their trade as to make it necessary to build more close and to live in towns."[2]

"Answer to No. 18.—*Christenings; to* No. 19.—*Marriages;* to No. 20,—*Burials;* to No. 26.—*Religion* and to No. 27 *Churches.*[3]

Secondly—That having as yet no further divisions of the said Province than into Counties, nor in truth any possibility of making as yet any further subdivisions into Parishes for the reasons before given, there is no way to be found to make calculations to satisfy these inquiries without taking a very great time and making such scrutinies

---
[1] Arch. Md., Vol. 5, p. 129.
[2] Arch. Md., Vol. 5, p. 266.
[3] Arch. Md., Vol. 5, p. 129.

as would certainly either endanger insurrections or a general dispeopling of the Province which is at present in great peace and quiet, all persons there being secured to their content for quiet enjoyment of everything that they can reasonably desire.

The reasons why such scrutinies would be thus dangerous is that vizt That at the first planting of the Province by my father albeit he had an absolute liberty given to him and his heirs to carry thither any persons of any of the Dominions that belonged to the Crown of England who should be found willing to go thither; yet when he came to make use of this liberty he found very few who were included to go and seat themselves in those parts but such as for some reason or other could not live with ease in other places. And of these a great part were such as could not conform in all particulars to the several laws of England relating to Religion.

Many there were of this sort of people who declared their willingness to go and plant themselves in this Province so as they might have a General Toleration settled there by a law by which all of all sorts who professed Christianity in general might be at liberty to worship God in such manner as was most agreeable with their respective judgments and consciences without being subject to any penalties whatsoever for their so doing provided the civil peace were preserved. And that for the securing the civil peace and preventing all heats feuds which were generally observed to happen amongst such as differ in opinions upon occasion of reproachful nicknames and reflecting upon each others opinions it might by the same law be made penal to give any offence in that kind, these were the conditions proposed by such as were willing to go and be the first planters of the Province. And without the complying with these conditions in all probability this Province had never been planted.

To these conditions my father agreed and accordingly soon after the first planting of this Province these conditions by the unanimous consent of all who were concerned were passed into a law and the inhabitants of this Province have found such effects from this law and from the strict observance of it, as well in relation to their quiet as in relation to the farther peopling of the Province that they look on it as that whereon alone depends the preservation of their peace, their properties and their liberties.

This being the true state of the case of this Province it is easy to judge what consequences might ensue upon any scrutinies which should be made in order to the satisfying these particular inquiries."[1]

Arch. Md., Vol. 5, pp. 267–9.

ADDRESS TO KING WILLIAM III.

"The address of the Representatives of their Majestie's[1] Protestant Subjects in the Province of Maryland assembled.

To the Kings most excellent Majestie—[2]

Whereas we are with all humility fully assured that the benefitt of your Majestie's glorious undertakings, and blessed success for the Protestant Religion, and civil rights and liberties of your Subjects, was graciously intended to be extensive as well to this remote part, as to all others of your Majestie's Territorys and Countreys, being thereby influenced to express our utmost zeal and endeavors for your Majestie's service and the Protestant Religion, here of late notoriously opposed, and your Majestie's sovereign dominion and Right to this your Majestie's Province of Maryland invaded and undermined by our late Popish Governors their Agents and Complices.

Wee your Majestie's most dutifull and loyall Subjects of the said Province being assembled as the Representative Body of the same; doe humbly pray your Majestie's graceous consideration of the great grievances and expressions wee have long layne under, lately represented to your Majestie and directed to your Majestie's principall Secretary of State, in a certain Declaration from the Commanders, Officers and Gentlemen in Armes for your Majestie's service and defence of the Protestant Religion.

And that your Majesty would be graciously pleased in such waies and methods as to your

[1] Arch. Md., Vol. 13, p. 239.
[2] Why was Queen Mary left out?

Princely wisdom shall seem meete, to appoynt such a deliverance to your suffering People, whereby for the future, our religion, rights and libertyes may be secured under a Protestant Government by your gracious direction specially to be appointed.

Wee will waite with all becoming duty and loyalty your Majestie's pleasure herein, and will in the mean time (to the hazard of our lives and fortunes) persevere and continue to vindicate and defend your Majestie's rights and soveraigne Dominion over this Province, the Protestant Religion and the Civil Rights and libertys of your Majestie's Subjects here against all manner of attempts and oppositions whatsoever, Hereby unanimously declaring that as we have a full sense of the blessings of heaven upon your Majestie's generous undertakeings, soe we will endeavor to express our due gratitude for the same as becomes Professors of the best of Religions, and Subjects to the best of Princes.[1]

Maryland—dated in the Assembly
sitting at the State House in the City of
St Maryes the 4th day of Septr 1689
in the first year of their Majestie's reign."

Endorsed

"Maryland
4th Septr 1689

Address of the Assembly to the King
Rec$^{'d}$ 31 Decr 1689."[2]

---

[1] Bernard C. Steiner says "they ask to be made a royal province." See "The Protestant Revolution in Maryland." Reports Am. Hist. Assoc., 1897.

[2] There are those who doubt the sincerity of this appeal to establish the Church of England in the Province of Maryland but the personnel of the Assembly of 1689 leads me to believe that the appeal was an honest expression of a desire for relief from a difficult situation.

INSTRUCTIONS TO GOV. LIONEL COPLEY[1,2]
August 26th, 1691.

"Where being arrived you are forthwith to call together the Members of our Councill for that our Province and Territory By name,

>Sir Thomas Lawrence K^t. and Bar^t.,
>Henry Jowles
>Nehemiah Blackiston
>Nicholas Greenbury
>Charles Hutchins
>Charles Robotham
>David Browne
>Thomas Tench
>John Addison
>John Coates
>James Frisby
>and
>Thomas Brooks, Esq.

And that God Almighty may be more inclined to bestow his blessing upon us and you in the welfare and improvement of that our Province you shall take especiall care that He be devoutly and duly served within your Government, the Book of Common Prayer as it is now established Read each Sunday and holiday and the blessed Sacrament administered according to the Rites of the Church of England.

You shall take care that the Churches already built there shall be well and orderly kept and more built as the Colony shall by God's blessing be improved and that besides a competent maintenance to be assigned to the Minister of each Church a convenient house be built at the common charge for each Minister.

[1] Arch. Md., Vol. 8, p. 271.
[2] Arch. Md., Vol. 8, p. 276. See also Commission of Gov. Lionel Copley.

You are not to preferr any Minister to any Ecclesiasticall Benefice in that Our Province without a Certificate from the Right Reverend the Bishop of London of his being conformable to the doctrine and discipline of the Church of England of a good life and conversation, And if any Person already preferred shall appear to you to give scandall either by his doctrine or manners you are to use the best means for the removall of him and to supply the vacancy in such manner as we have directed.

And you are to give Order forthwith if the same be not already done, that every Orthodox Minister within your Government be one of the Vestry in his respective Parish and that no vestry be held without him except in case of sickness or that after notice of a vestry summoned he absent himself.

And you are to enquire whether there be any Minister within your Government who Preaches and Administers the Sacrament in any Orthodox Church or Chapel without being in due Orders, whereof you are to give an account to the said Bishop of London.

And to the end the Eccliasticall Jurisdiction of the said Bishop of London may take place in that our Province as far as conveniently may be We do think fit that you give all countenance and Encouragement in the exercise of the same excepting *only* the Colating to Benefices, Granting Licenses for Marriage and Probate of Wills, which we have reserved to you our Governor or the Commander-in-Chief for the time being."

ASSOCIATORS—1690

Capt. John Coode
Commander

St. Mary's County	Kenelm Cheseldyne
	Nehemiah Blackiston
Kent County	Michael Miller
	William Harris
Anne Arundel	Nicholas Gassaway
	Nicholas Greenbury
Calvert	Henry Jowles
	Ninian Beale
Charles	John Addison
	John Court (Coates)
Baltimore	John Thomas
	Thos. Staley
Talbot	Geo. Robotham
	John Edmondson
Somerset	David Browne
	Robert King
Dorchester	John Brooke
	Henry Trippe
Cecil	Edward Jones
	Charles James.

Of the Associators, Blackiston, Robotham, Jowles, Addison, Browne, Court and Greenbury were made members of the Council by Gov. Lionel Copley, and Cheseldyne, Harris, Staley, Edmondson, Trippe, Brooke and Jones were elected members of the Provincial Assembly in 1692.

[1] Arch. Md.. Vol. 8, p. 199.

THE COUNCIL AND ASSEMBLY
May 10th–June 9th, 1692.

During this period the "Act for the Service, etc." was passed.

Lionel Copley, Esq., Governor.

Council

Col. Nehemiah Blackiston Col. David Browne
    Speaker Capt. John Court (Coates)
Col. George Robotham Mr. Thos. Brooke
Col. Charles Hutchins Col. Nicholas Greenbury
Col. Henry Jowles Mr. Thos. Tench
Capt. John Addison Mr. James Frisby
Sir Thomas Lawrence, Bart.

John Llewellin
Clerk to Council.[1]

Assembly

Speaker—Mr. Kenelm Cheseldyne [2]

St. Mary's City
  Edw. Wynne, Esq.
  Mr. Robert Mason
St. Mary's County
  Mr. Kenelm Cheseldyne
  Maj. John Carvell
  Mr. Philip Clarke
  Mr. John Watson
Kent County
  Mr. Wm. Harris
  Mr. Hans Hanson
  Mr. Elias King
  Mr. Saml. Wheeler

Baltimore County
  Mr. Geo. Ashman
  Mr. Edw. Boothby
  Mr. Fra. Watkins
  Mr. Thos. Staley
Talbot County
  Mr. Robert Smith
  Mr. Wm. Phiney (Finney)
  Mr. Hugh Sherwood
  Mr. John Edmondson
Somerset County
  Capt. Wm. Whittington
  Rev. John Hewett

[1] Arch. Md., Vol. 13, p. 252.
[2] Arch. Md., Vol. 13, p. 350.

THE FIRST PARISHES OF THE PROVINCE OF MARYLAND 41

Anne Arundel County
Mr. John Hammond
Mr. Henry Ridgeley
Mr. James Sanders
Mr. John Dorsey
Calvert County
Mr. Thomas Greenfield
Mr. Thomas Tasker
Mr. Henry Mitchell
Mr. John Bigger
Charles County
Mr. Wm. Dent
Mr. Henry Hawkins
Maj. Ja. Smallwood
Capt. Philip Hoskins

Mr. Thomas Evernden
Mr. John Godden
Dorchester County
Maj. Henry Trippe
Dr. John Brooke
Mr. Thos. Ennalls
Mr. Edw. Pinder
Cecil County
Mr. William Dare
Col. St. Leger Codd
Mr. Edward Jones
Mr. George Warner

Henry Denton
Clerk to the House.

Changes in Personnel.

"Came the speaker of the House and prayed his Excellencys Order for the Issueing out of Writts of Election of Burgesses to serve in the room [place] of Mr John Edmondson of Talbot County, Mr Everdine [Evernden], Mr Godwin and Mr Huett of Somerset County Mr Warner, Mr Dare and Col. Codd of Cecil County disabled and Expelled the House, which was granted."[1]

Mr. Thomas Everdine and Mr. John Edmondson being Quakers refused to take the Oaths.[2] Mr. John Godwin was a Quaker.[3]

Mr. Huett (Hewett) was "dismissed the House by reason of his Ministerial function, the Law in that Case as was

[1] Arch. Md., Vol. 13, p. 268.
[2] Arch. Md., Vol. 13, p. 253.
[3] Arch. Md., Vol. 13, p. 354.

afore desired being read in the house, rendering him, in the Opinion of the whole house, unqualified."[1]

On May 14th, 1692, Mr. Huett and the Rev. James Clayland, later rector of St. Michael's Parish, Talbot County, were asked to serve as Chaplains to the Assembly and answered that they "will be ready at the State house every Morning, to say Divine Service upon the Beate of the second Drume, dureing this Sessions of Assembly."[2] Their salaries were fixed at 3000 lbs. of Tobacco.

Mr. Huett was rector of Stepney Church and of Old Monie in Somerset.

The cause for dismissal of Col. St. Leger Codd and Mr. George Warner of Cecil was found by the Committee in the fact that they "called Cecil County Court [in April, 1690] and held the same in the name of the Lord Baltimore, denying the Authority of the Late Convention, etc."[3]

Mr. Wm. Dare was permitted to take his seat providing he give security for his good behavior. Upon his refusal to give the required security he was ordered to appear for contempt. He finally, upon giving some excuse, was permitted to pay a fine of 200 pounds of Tobacco and be discharged from custody of the "Serjeant att Armes."[4]

Mr. James Wroth, Mr. Robert Crooke and Mr. Thomas Theakston were elected to serve in the Assembly for Cecil County, "in the Roome of Col. Codd, Mr Warner and Mr Dare." . . . "accordingly the oaths appointed by Act of Parliament instead of the Oaths of Allegiance and Supremacy were administered to the aforesaid members" on May the 27th, 1692.[5]

[1] Arch. Md., Vol. 13, p. 366.
[2] Arch. Md., Vol. 13, p. 367.
[3] Arch. Md., Vol. 13, p. 365.
[4] Arch. Md., Vol. 13, p. 368.
[5] Arch. Md., Vol. 13, pp. 366–397.

"Came from the House Mr Whittington and Mr Ennals and desired to have the Sheriff's Return of the new Election for Somerset County. . . . Said Whittington and Ennals came again for the House together with Mr Roger Woolford, Mr John Bozman and Mr Lawrence Mattox members returned for Somerset County . . . they were accordingly sworn and dismist" June the 2nd, 1692.[1]

"The Sheriff of Talbot County makes return of Mr Thomas Robins a delegate chosen for the said County in this Assembly in the Room of Mr John Edmondson disabled and dismissed the House."[2]

---

[1] Arch. Md., Vol. 13, p. 327.
[2] Arch. Md., Vol. 13, p. 326.

ALL LAWS REPEALED
—1692—

"An Act of Repeale of all Laws heretofore made in this Province and confirming all Laws made this Generall Assembly.

Be it Enacted by the King and Queens Most Excellent Majesties by and with the advice and consent of this present Generall Assembly.

That all Laws heretofore made in this Province be and forever hereby stand Repealed annulled and void, and that all Laws now made and assented to this present Generall Assembly (and no other) be and remain in full force and power according to the true intent and meaning thereof and that the same be accounted and esteemed as the body of the Laws of this Province and no other heretofore made.

Provided always that this Law shall not extend or be Construed to make void any persons Right by Acts of nature Affections on any private Acts heretofore made relating to any private persons, but that the same be hereby kept and preserved to them according to the true intent and meaning thereof anything herein to the Contrary notwithstanding.[1]

June 7th, 1692.
Assented to by the Councill
Board
Signed p Ord^r
W. Taylard Clk.
Assistant

June the 7th 1692
The house of Assembly
have Assented
Signed p Ord^r
Hen: Denton Clk:"

---

[1] Arch. Md., Vol. 13, p. 560.

PART III.

THE FIRST LAW ESTABLISHING THE CHURCH

FIRST LAW ESTABLISHING THE CHURCH

"AN ACT FOR THE SERVICE OF ALMIGHTY GOD AND THE ESTABLISHMENT OF THE PROTESTANT RELIGION WITHIN THIS PROVINCE."

Act of Assembly at a session held at St. Mary's 1692

Lionel Copley, Esq.
Royal Governor.

It was under this law that the parishes of the Provinces were laid out.

The first record of any action taken by the Assembly to establish the Church of England in the Province of Maryland is found in the proceedings of that body under date of May 16th, 1692. It follows:

"Ordered that the following Articles be drawne up into Lawes vizt—

> Article No. 1. That the number of Ordinaries be ascertained in each County.
>
> Article No. 2. To Lay the Province into Parishes and that care be taken for provision for the Clergy."[1]

. . . .

Two days later, May 18th, the bill had been drawn up, "read and passed the lower house the first reading with some amendments to be referred."

On the 25th of May the following note is found in Assembly Proceedings:

[1] Arch. Md., Vol. 13, p. 368 and 369.

"The Act Concerning Religion they think most proper to Consider of and make provision for Glebes when the Parishes are settled and laid out."

The Council read the bill for the first time on the next day (May 26th) and, after making the customary notations as to reading, the following "Remark" was added:

"The Ministers to be one of the Vestry according to his Excellency's Instructions and a Clause to be incerted Empowering the Vestrymen with the Advice and Assistance of the Commissioners to purchase and procure one or more Glebes in a County and in such places as there shall be occasion, or they shall be Convenient vizt One Glebe in a Parish each Glebe to Consist of fifty Acres of Land at the least and not under."[1]

The bill received its second reading in the Council on the 27th of May and was sent to the Assembly. The Lower House adding the following:

"Signify the opinion of the House thereupon that it may not commence nor take force till March next."[2]

The same day it also received a reading in the Lower House brought from the Council. The following is an extract upon the records:

"An Act for the Service, etc., ordered to be read, upon which was reassumed a former Vote concerning the Settlement of an Annuall Income in each parish upon the Ministry within the Province and Voted whether it should be done by the Assessmen^t of Forty or 20 ^{lbs} of tob$^{o.}$ p. poll, and Carryed by the Majority of Voices to be assessed by a Taxe of Forty pounds of Tobacco p. poll upon the Taxeables of each parish."[3]

Under date of June the 2nd the following record shows the work completed and ready for the Governor's signature.

[1] Arch. Md., Vol. 13, p. 306.
[2] Arch. Md., Vol. 13, f. 316.
[3] Arch. Md., Vol. 13, p. 396.

"An Act for the Service of Almighty God, &c thus subscribed, vizt
June the 2$^{nd.}$ 1692
The House of Assembly have assented
Signed p Order
Henry Denton Clk
Read here and Subscribed June the 2$^{nd.}$ 1692
Assented to by the Council
Signed p order
J. Llewellin Clk"[1]

Governor Copley on June the 9th "desired the House would walke up and see the Lawes signed." "Mr Speaker with the Rest of the Members of the House goe up to the Councill Chamber accordingly where were signed by the Governor and passed under the Great Seale of the Province the following Lawes, vizt
An Act for the Service, etc"[2]

"Maryland S. S.[3]

Att an Assembly held at the Citty of S$^{t.}$ Mary's on the Tenth Day of May Anno Dom. 1692. And in the 4th Year of the Reign of Our Soveraign Lord & Lady William and Mary by the Grace of God of England Scotland France and Ireland King and Queen &c^a These Acts following were made.

. . . .

[Title.]

An Act for the Service of Almighty God and the Establishment of the Protestant Religion within this Province

[1] Arch. Md., Vol. 13, p. 328.
[2] Arch. Md., Vol. 13, p. 421.
[3] Arch. Md., Vol. 13, p. 425.

[Preamble.]

Foreasmuch as in a well Governed Commonwealth Matters of Religion and the Honour of God ought in the first place to be taken in serious consideration, and nothing being more acceptable to Almighty God than the true and Sincere worship and Service of him according to his Holy Word.

I. *Bee it therefore Enacted* by the King and Queens most Excellent Majestys by and with the advice and consent of this present General Assembly and the Authority of the same

[Rights of the Church of England.]

That the Church of England within this Province shall have and Enjoy all her Rights Liberties and Franchises wholly inviolable as is now or shall be hereafter Established by Law, and also that the Great Charter of England be kept and observed in all points—

[Sunday Observances.]

—and forasmuch as the sanctifying and keeping holy of the Lords Day commonly called Sunday is and hath been Esteemed by the present and all primitive Churches and People a Principall and Chief part of the said Worship, which Day in most places of this Province hath been and still is by many wicked Lewd and disorderly people Prophaned and neglected, by working Drunkeness Swearing Gaming & other unlawful pastimes and debaucheries, for remedy whereof, for the future—

[Penalty for Sabbath breaking.]

II. *Bee it Enacted* by the King and Queens most Excellent Majestys and by and with the advice and consent aforesaid, That from and after the publication of this Law no Person or Persons within this province shall work or do any bodily Labour or Occupation upon any Lord's Day commonly called Sunday, etc.,[1] . . .

[Establishing the Church of England.]
And for the raising of a Supply of the Ministry and the Maintenance of the ministers of Gods word and Sacraments—

[Meeting of Commissioners and Justices of each County.]
III. *Bee it Enacted* by the Authority aforesaid that the severall Commissioners and Justices of each respective county within this Province shall at some convenient time between this and the first day of September next ensuing, meet together—

[Place of Meeting.]
At the respective places of holding Courts for the same Countys,

[Freeholders notified to attend the meetings.]
—and shall give notice to the most principal Freeholders[2] of the severall Counties to attend them at the said time and place of meeting to be by the said Commissioners and Justices appointed, ten days before the same—

[Dividing the Counties into Parishes.]
—and thereby and with the advice of the Principal freeholders aforesaid so many of them as the said Commissioners and Justices shall call to their Assistance divide and lay out their severall and respective Counties into severall districts and Parishes—

---

[1] Considerable space taken up here with penalties for drunkeness, etc., on Sunday.
[2] "Freeholder (Principal Freeholder) entitled to vote or to represent county in General Assembly must have a freehold of fifty acres of land or a visible estate of Forty pounds Sterling at the least." (Md. Arch., Vol. 27, pp. 352–1708.)

[Number of Parishes to each County.]

—so many as the conveniency of each respective county and the scituation of the same will afford and allow of, as in the discretion of the said Justices with the advice aforesaid shall be thought convenient.

[Parish boundaries to be well defined.]

And the same districts and Parishes the said Justices shall cause to be laid out by meets and Bounds and fair certificats of each Parish with the most evident and demonstrable Bounds of the same, return to the next County Court to be held for the said County,—

[Parish boundaries recorded in County Records.]

—which the Justices at their County Courts as aforesaid shall cause the Clerk of the said Court to enter the said certificate uppon Record,—

[Copy of Parish Certificate sent to the Governor.]

—and draw a fair Copy thereof, affixing his name and the Seale of said County thereunto and Transmitt the same with all convenient speed to the Govr and Councill of this Province to be kept on Record in the Councill Books,—

[Clerks fee for recording.]

—for which the said Clerk shall be allowed as for other matters recorded to be paid by the severall counties,—

[Penalties.]

—and for the more sure and certaine Effecting of the same, the severall Justices of the severall Counties within this Province, which Clerks aforesaid are hereby enjoyned and required to do and perform the severall Injunctions requisite and parts of this Law under the penalty of five hundred pounds of Tobacco to every Justice failing in the premisses, and to the Clerk one thousand pounds of Tobacco—

[Fines in their Majestie's names.]
　—to be recovered in their Majestie's names in any Court of Record in this Province—

[Fines applied to Parish use.]
　—and Employed to the use of the Parrish where the said offender shall reside—

[Meeting held to choose Vestries.]
　—and the Severall Parishes being laid out *limited and bounded in the severall Counties* within this Province as aforesaid the Freeholders of each Parish do within some convenient time within two months—

[Justices to appoint time and place of meeting.]
　—as by the Justices of County Courts aforesaid shall be appointed, meet together at the most convenient place in the said Parish to be appointed by the Justices aforesaid,—

[Six vestrymen to be chosen.]
　—and there make choice of six of the most able men of the said respective Parishes to be a Vestry for each respective Parish as aforesaid,—

[Vestrymen given authority of office.]
　—who are hereby Authorized Impowered and required to take care of preserve and Imploy all such Tobaccos,

Wares, goods and Merchandizes as by this Act or any other Act hereafter to be made, or by any other waies or means whatsoever shall be given or granted raised or allowed to the use of the Church or Ministry of the said Parish to which they belong.

[Vestry meeting to take account of parish income.]

To which end and purpose the said Vestrymen or the Major part of them when and as often as need shall require shall meet together and have a Clerk[1] to attend them to take the accompt of all such Tobaccos, Goods, Wares and Merchandizes as by any means as aforesaid shall accrue to the use of the Ministry in the Parish aforesaid,—

[To build churches and chapel.]

—and with the first Tobaccos, goods Wares and Merchandizes as aforesaid, shall erect and build in the most convenient place of the said Parish, one Church or Chappell—

[Vestrymen to decide on dimensions, etc.]

—in such Dimentions and Proportions and in such Methods and ways as by the said Vestry men in their discretion and Judgement shall think fitt and convenient—

[Exceptions where churches are already built.]

—(such Parishes as already at the time of the laying out of the same shall appear to have churches and Chappells already built in them Excepted)—

[Vestrymen to keep record.]

—the said Vestry men alwayes keeping a Record how and in what manner they shall execute and performe the severall Trusts in this Act reposed in them—

---

[1] Clerk to Vestry.

[Vestry to obtain a yearly list of taxables in their parish.]
—and also shall procure yearly and every year from the Constables within each hundred within their Parishes aforesaid or by such other waies or means as to them shall seem expedient a true & just accompt and list of all Taxable Persons within their Parish aforesaid—

[List of taxables kept with vestry records.]
—and the same yearly and every year cause to be recorded amongst their other Proceedings, the better to Enable them to know what sum or sums of Tobac° to demand and require of the Sherriff of the County for the use of their Parish aforesaid, as by this Act hereafter shall be raised for the uses aforesaid,—

[Tax of forty pounds of tobacco.]
That is to say, That a Tax or assessment of forty pounds of tobacco per poll be yearly and in every year raised and levyed upon every Taxable Person within each Parrish aforesaid,—

[Sheriff to collect "Forty per poll."]
—and to be collected and gathered by the Sherriff of the County in manner and form as the publick or County Levies hitherto have and still are collected and gathered—

[Sheriff to pay the tax to the vestrymen.]
—which said Sherriff is to make punctuall payment of the said Tax or Assessment to the Vestrymen of each Parrish as aforesaid, of so much Tobacco as by the Tax aforesaid shall be raised within each Parrish,—

[Sheriff's commission for collecting tax.]
—the said Sherriff deducting his Salary for collecting the same, five pounds of Tobacco per cent,—

[How tax shall be applied.]

—which said Tobacco so Assessed and raised as aforesaid shall always and after the building of the Church or Chappell within the each Parrish as aforesaid be appropriated and applyed by the Vestrymen aforesaid to the use and benefit of the Minister of that Parrish if any Minister [be] Inducted into the same,—

[Tax to be spent for repairs when there is no minister.]

—But if no Minister be Inducted into the Parish, then the same Tobacco or such part thereof as by the said Vestry men shall be thought convenient to be kept and made use on for the necessary reparations of the Church or Chappell aforesaid or other pious uses at the discretion of the Vestry men aforesaid.

[Vestrymen authorized to accept donations to the church.]

And to the end that any gift bequest Grant ordination or appointment by any person or persons which shall be so piously inclined either by their last Wills and Testaments or by Deed Executed in their life time to give grant or anyways appoint or bestow any sum or sums of Money Tobaccos Goods or Chattells Lands Tenements or hereditaments of what nature or kind soever for the use and benefit of any Minister or Ministers or to the Ministry or Poor of any Parrish or Parrishes within this Province, the Vestrymen for the same Parrish by this Act are Impowered and Authorized to take the same into their Custody and Possession and apply to the use and intent of the Donor or Donors—

[Vestry authorized to sue.]

And the better to enable them to recover and receive the same, they are hereby fully and absolutely Empoweerd

Authorized and Qualified to prosecute and maintain any Action or Actions whatsoever, whether reall personall or mixt for the Recovery of all or any the premisses aforesaid from any Person or persons that shall hold or deteine any of the goods or chattles Tenements or hereditaments as aforesaid, given and granted & otherwise appointed to the uses aforesaid, or for any damages accruing by any Trespass upon and in the premisses or any of them,—

[Vestrymen to act as "body corporate."]

—and in the Prosecution of any Action or accōns as aforesaid to prosecute Act and do in the nature and amply as a body Politick or corporate might or could do for the recovering of the same and preserving of the premisses aforesaid—

[Suits to be entered in name of the principal vestryman with the other vestrymen.]

—in any Action or Actions to be comēnced as aforesaid in the Writt and Declaration and other proceedings of the same the principall Vestryman shall be named together with the other his Vestrymen as aforesaid for the Parrish especially appointed by Act of Assembly any Law Statute or useage to the contrary hereof in any wise notwithstanding.

[Vestrymen to fill vacancies in vestry.]

And when any Vestryman or Vestrymen shall at any time hereafter happen to dy or depart this life or out of the Parish to which he or they belonged, It shall and may be lawfull to the other Vestrymen who are hereby enjoyned at their next meeting to make choice of such other able person or persons residing and being Freeholders in the

Parrish aforesaid to make up the number of such deceased absent Vestryman or Vestrymen as aforesaid.

[Date that Act shall become effective.]

This Act as to the raising and Assessing a Support by the Poll not to commence or be in force untill after the Tenth Day of March [1693] next, but as to all other parts thereof, from and after the Publication of the same.

June 2nd 1692	June 2nd 1692
Assented to by the Council Board.	The house of Assembly have Assented
Signed p Ord^r	Signed p Ord^r
John Llewellin Clk.	Hen: Denton Clk."

"The aforesaid Law was signed and Subscribed by the Governor thus vizt
June 9th 1692

On behalfe of their Maj^{ties} King W^m and Queen Mary I will these to be laws.

L. Copley."[1]

---

[1] Arch. Md., Vol. 13, p. 424. This Act was repealed by the Act of 1696, same title.

TAXABLES

"An Act for the Constables Taking a List of Taxables.

—And to the end that no person for the future may be Ignorant what Persons are Taxables and what not
   Be it Enacted by and with the Advice and Consent aforesaid and the Authority of the same, That all Male Children born within this Province and Resident in it shall be taken and Accompted Taxables at the Age of sixteen years and upwards, and all male Children Servants Imported into this Province at the age of sixteen years and upwards shall be accompted Taxables, And all Slaves whatsoever, whether Male or Female Imported or born in this Province at or above the Age of sixteen years shall be accompted Taxables and so Rated, And that all freemen within this Province (Except Clergymen and such poor & Impotent persons that receive Alms from the County) shall be Taxables above the Age of Sixteen years.

June 2nd 1692   June the 2nd 1692
Signed p. Ord^r The House of Assembly have
John Llewellin Clk   Assented
                                       Signed p. Ord^r
                                       Hen: Denton Clk."[1]

---

[1] Arch. Md., Vol. 13, p. 538. Assembly proceedings.

SHERIFF'S JURISDICTION.

"At a Council held at Port of Annapolis.
March 3ᵈ 1695.

The Question:

Ordered that it be referred to Mr Attorney & Solicitor Generall whether the Sherriffs now at present Officiating & Acting in the late divided Counties can legally continue to Act in their several places, in the Counties as (by the late Law) they stand now divided, and whether the Commissions of the peace &c^a ought not to issue, and that they make Report of their opinion therein unto this Board with all speed; who make the following Return vizt

The Opinion:

We humbly conceive that after the day in the Act of Assembly mentioned for dividing the Counties, the Sheriff of each County is *not* to Act beyond the limits of the County in the Act mentioned, and for prevention of inconveniency and for the better administering Justice, it would be requisite that the Commission to All Officers Judiciall & Ministeriall should be made to take Effect at that time, in the new Erected County.

        (Signed)   Geo: Plater [Attorney General]
        (Signed)   Wm. Dent"[1] [Solicitor General]

---

[1] Arch. Md., Vol. 20, p. 380. This opinion is quoted here to impress upon the reader the fact that the boundaries of parishes and counties were official and that the map (in back of book) of the province showing those boundaries is based upon that opinion. In other words the parish boundaries were made co-extensive with the country boundaries.

PART IV.

INSTRUCTIONS TO VESTRYMEN

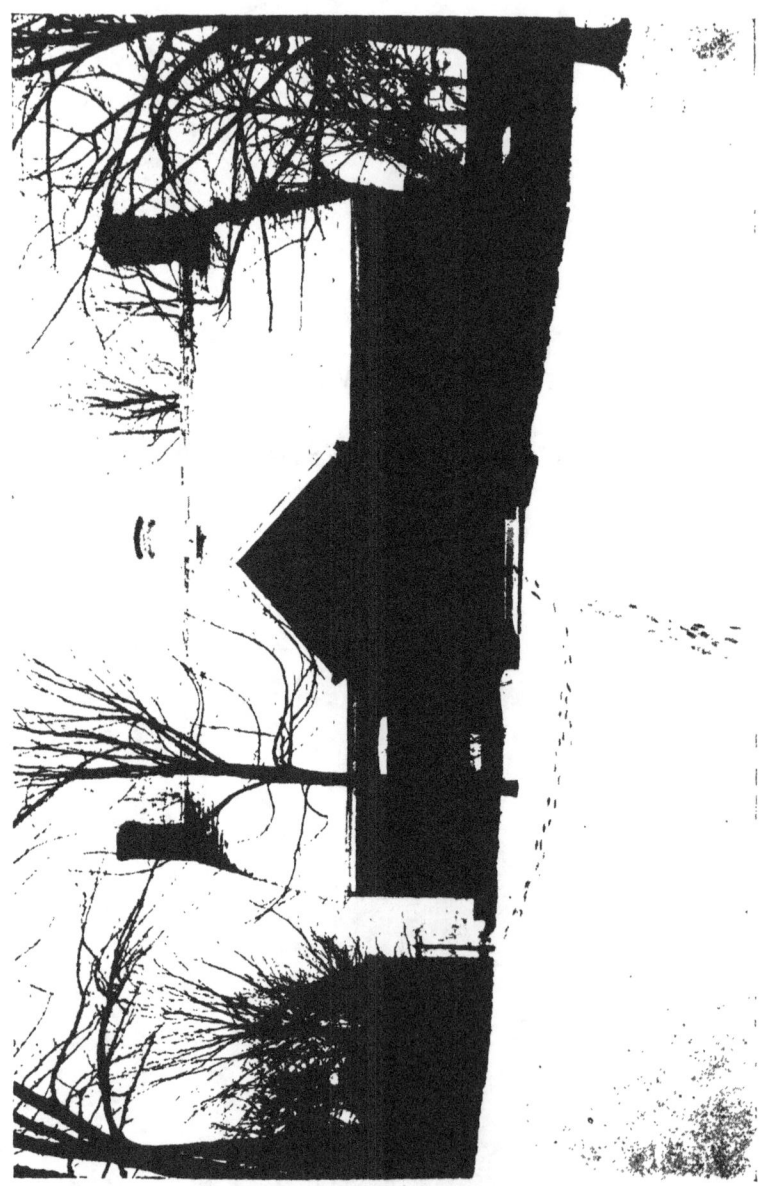

OLD COUNCIL HOUSE

Here the law of 1702 governing the Church of England in the Province of Maryland was signed.

INSTRUCTIONS TO VESTRYMEN

By
"His Ex^ncy Francis Nicholson, Esq., Capt Gen^ll &^ca"
And his Councellors

Shortly after the passage of the "Act for the Service of Almighty God and the Establishment of the Protestant Religion within this Province" the Governor and Council issued instructions to the Vestrymen throughout the Province.

There were many things to learn in the management of the affairs of the Church under the *Act of 1692* and no doubt the vestrymen were glad to be instructed on such important questions.

"At a Council held at the Port of Annapolis
March 4th 1695

Order touching the Vestry's, what inside Worke they are obliged to perform in their Churches

Upon Representation, Ordered that the Vestrymen of the severall and respective Parishes within this Province be obliged to perform & see finished, within their respective parish Churches, no other inside worke than Viz^t plastering the Walls, making the pulpit, the Reading pew & Clerks Desk, to provide a Communion table & Raile in the same; And as for all other pews & seats, that the severall Parishioners be at charge of making the same according to their own liking. And it is hereby further ordered that the Sheriffs of the Province give Copy of this Order to the severall Vestrys within their respective Precincts."[1]

"At a Council held at the Port of Annapolis
August 17th 1695.
Vestrymen Ordered to build Churches, &c[a] [2]

[Vestrymen to build churches where needed.]

Ordered that the Vestrymen of the Severall and Respective parishes within this Province take all due and Speedy care for the building of Churches (where wanting)—

[Oathes and test for vestrymen.]

—and for the taking the Oathes & Subscribing to the Test—

[Choosing church wardens.]

—as also chooseing Church Wardens pursuant to the directions of the Act of Assembly of this Province in that Case made & provided;

[County court houses to be used as churches.]

And that where the Court houses within any of the Counties of the Province are placed convenient where Churches may stand or be Erected, that in such case said the Court houses may be made use of for Churches to perform Divine Duty & Service in;

[1] Arch. Md., Vol. 20, p. 388.
[2] Arch. Md., Vol. 20, p. 283.

[Dorchester County Court House.]
—especially Dorchester County Court house in the parish of Great Choptanck, so that instead of Building a church at Cambridge, the Vestrey may build a Chappell of Ease in some other Convenient place,

[This rule to be observed in other parishes.]
And in like manner other parishes are hereby directed and Required to Observe and follow the same Rule.

[Appointment of Lay Readers in vacant parishes.]
And it is hereby further Ordered, that where ministers are wanting in any the said parishes the Vestreymen for the same appointed take care to provide some sober, discreet person to Read prayers on Sundays,

[Lay Readers appointed to assist ministers of two parishes.]
And where it so falls out that one Minister happens to Enjoy the benefits & profits of two parishes that then such Minister provide some sober and discreet person to Read prayers as aforesaid in that Church those days the minister shall therein be absent, Provided the whole Forty per poll be paid such Minister, Requireing such persons diligently to observe the Reading the first & second Service & the people to stand and kneele as the Rubrick directs;

[Care of Churches.]
And that the churches be decently kept & the Communion Tables Raild in,

[Baptism of children after reading of Second Lesson.]
And Further Ordered that all Children brought to Church to be baptized be Christened immediately after the Reading of the Second Lesson

[Administering the Lord's Supper.]

—& that the Holy Sacrament of the Lords Supper be administered at least three times every year, Viz^t Christmas, Easter & Whitsontide;

[Collecting the "Forty per poll."]

And that where the Forty per poll was not Collected last year that the same be Collected this year (according to the Directions of the Order of the last Assembly) for the Use of the Ministry, Ministers being sent for in and Expected this Fall;

[Sheriff to report to the Governor & Council on property given to the church.]

And lastly Ordered that the Severall Sherriffes of the province make Strict inquiry of the Justices or other persons living within their respective Counties, if there be any Glebe Lands or personall Estate bestowed or given to the Church or towards building of Schooles or other pious Uses, whereof the Sherriffes are to Return an Account unto this Board—

[Sheriff to notify vestry of this order.]

—& give Copy of this Order to the Vestry of each parish within their respective County's and that they signify to this Board under their hand by the 2^d day of October next of their having so done, under the pain & perill which may Ensue for neglect of the same;—
Sheriffs to report number of taxables.

The list of Taxables are then likewise by you to be Return'd."

"At a Council held at the Port of Annapolis
August 20th 1695
[Churches to be used as Court Houses.]

Ordered that it be Recommended to the house of Burgesses for a Law to be made that the Church at Mount Calvert be fitted to serve as well for a Court house as Church, and so in all other places where the same can conveniently be done."[1]

"At a Council held at the Port of Annapolis[2]
October 10th 1696"

[Order to the Vestrys to dispose of the "Forty per poll.]

Ordered that the Vestrys of the Severall parishes within this Province take care to dispose of the 40 p poll (where Ministers are not placed or inducted and where Churches are actually built) for ready Goods, Money or bills of Exchange pursuant to Former Ord^r Tobacco being a good com̄odity this Year; and that the Church Yards be pail'd pursuant to the late Ordinance of Assembly the Sherriffs being hereby directed to give a Copy of this Order to the Severall Vestrys within their respective Bayliwicks."

"At a Council held at the Port of Annapolis[3]
October 10th 1696.

[Returns of County Levys and Vestry Proceedings.]

Ordered that the Clerks of the Severall County Courts and Vestrys make Return of their County Leavys and Vestry proceedings next December Court, and so from that time Annually pursuant to the late Act of Assembly, and that the Sherriffs give them notice thereof."

[1] Arch. Md., Vol. 20, p. 284.
[2] Arch. Md., Vol. 20, p. 523.
[3] Arch. Md., Vol. 20, p. 524.

"At a Council held at the Port of Annapolis [1]
December 16th 1696.

[Order to Vestrys to make return about the Churches.]

Ordered that the Vestrys of the respective parishes within this Province make Return what forwardness the Churches are in and whether Finished according to Contract and paid for, and whether the ground the same stand on is purchased & made secure to the parishion^{rs} to the End if it should not, and Act of Assembly may be procured for the Same, and that the Severall Vestrys have the s^d Accounts ready for his Ex^{ncys} perusall against he comes and visitts the s^d Churches, which (God willing) he intends very shortly and that the Sherriffs Serve them Severally with a Copy hereof."

---

[1] Arch. Md., Vol. 20, p. 584.

PART V.

THE LAW UNDER WHICH THE CHURCH OF ENGLAND FUNCTIONED UNTIL THE REVOLUTION IN 1775

Papers Relating to the Validity of the Law and the Act Providing for the Disposition of the Taxes

"AN ACT FOR THE ESTABLISHM^T OF RELIGIOUS WORSH^{PP} IN THIS PROVINCE ACCORDING TO THE CHURCH OF ENGLAND: AND FOR THE MAINTAINANCE OF MINISTERS."[1]

Act of Assembly—March 25th 1702.

The defects of the previous similar bills framed by the Assembly had caused their rejectment and upon the advice of Dr. Thomas Bray, who had fathered the Act of April 26th, 1700, and who had appeared personally in London before the Board of Trade and failed to get it passed; the Assembly asked the Commissioners of Trade and Plantation to prepare a bill that would be allowed by the Crown indicating their willingness to pass such as an Act of the Assembly of Maryland.

The defect in the Act of 1700 was the clause, "Bee it Enacted by the Authority aforesaid that the booke of Common Prayer and Admistration of the Sacraments with other Rites and Ceremonys of the Church According to the use of the Church of England the Psalter or Psalms of David and Morning and Evening Prayer therein contained be Solemnly read by *all* and *Every* Minister or Reader in *Every* Church or other *Place* of *Public Worship* within this Province."[2]

---

[1] Arch. Md., Vol. 24, p. 265. This is the Law under which the Church functioned for over seventy years.
[2] Arch. Md., Vol. 24, p. 91. For statement of Council in regard to restrictions see Letter to Commissioners of Trade and Plantation, page 166.

This deprived the Quakers and other dissenters of the benefits of toleration they had enjoyed. Upon receiving a letter from the "Right Honble the Lords of Plantation and Trade" notifying him of the failure to pass the Act of 1700, Governor Nathaniel Blackiston addressed the Council and Lower House in joint session on the 16th of March, 1702. He said in part:

> "The Law for Establishing religious worship in this Province according to the Church of England which you made last & sent home is now returned by his Majesty for your Assent. You'll find the Alterations, that are made but very little, and that such Visible Amendments to our Advantage being corrected by so wise an Hand. We ought to be proud of the pattern in confirming it. If I mistake not your Journalls of Assembly will make it appear that this Way was humbly *requested by yourselves* in an Address to his Majesty that *he would be pleased to order it to be drawn as he should judge fit and it be remitted to you for your Concurrence* and therefore since this Law was so unanimously made by you I have not the least doubt that any crafty Inclinations will abate your good Intentions in confirming so glorious and good an Act; But that you will cheerfully Join in putting it on foot His Majesty has been graciously pleased to give us an handle so to do. That for the future it may not be within the reach of our opponents to shock it again, tho their Efforts have proved feeble hitherto yet you ought not to trust any longer, but Endeavour to plant it firm to your Posterity which will be a most lasting Testimonie of your virtues."[1]

---

[1] Arch. Md., Vol. 24, p. 207.

On Tuesday, March 17th, 1702, the Governor sent the bill to the Lower House "for your Consideration, and your Concurrence and Resolutions thereon are desired with as much speed as conveniently may be."[1] Owing to the absence of several of the members of the Lower House, no action was taken until the 20th of March, at which time a full attendance of the members allowed the Assembly to proceed with its consideration. The Council records show that on the 20th "Came Major Dent and M^r [Edward] Lloyd from the House to desire a Conference of Some Members of their House with some Members of the Council upon the Bill proposed for Establishment of religious Worship within this Province, which Conference was readily granted when the House shall think fitt. Col. Addison, Col. Courts, Mr Brooke and Col. Hammond appointed to conferr with the members assigned by the House."

After the conference at the morning session, the bill was read the first time. A vote was then taken as to whether it should pass as it came from England. "Carryed in the affirmative and ordered that the blanks be filled up and it be th^s endorsed, *Resolved that it pass without any amendment* and ordered to be read ag^{ne} this afternoone."[2] It was read the second time in the Lower House and passed; it also received two readings and was "agreed to" by the Council at the same session and then sent up to the Committee to be engrossed.

At the Council meeting on Monday morning, March 23rd, 1702, the Governor read a part of a letter written to him by Dr. Thos. Bray, under date of July 15th, 1701. Doctor Bray called attention to the work he had done in England for the "Law of Religion" and says "My own Time and Pains in this affaire I willingly make an offering of together

[1] Arch. Md., Vol. 24, p. 209.
[2] Arch. Md., Vol. 24, p. 247.

with what other Services have been done the Country." He then states that he expected to be reimbursed for the outlay of cash (upwards of £50) paid out in soliciting the passage of the bill before the Board of Trade in England. A vote of thanks was tendered Doctor Bray by the Upper and Lower Houses and an order drawn to reimburse him for that which he had "disbursed in negotiating the said affair about the Act for Religious Worship."[1]

At the Afternoon session on March 23rd, the bill received its third reading in the Council and sent to the Lower House by Col. Addison and Mr. Brooke, where it received its final reading and approval.

"An Act for the Establishment of Religious Worship in this Province according to the Church of England and for the Maintainence of Ministers [2]

[March 25th 1702]

[Preamble.]

For as much as in well grounded Xpiom coṁon Wealths Matter concerning Religion and the honour of God ought in the First place, to be taken into consideration. And honest Endeavour to Attaine to such good end Countenanced and Encouraged as being not only most Acceptable to God; but the best way and Means to Obtaine his mercy and blessing upon a People or Country.

[Use of Book of Common Prayer authorized.]

I. *Be it therefore Enacted* by the Kings most Excellent Maj^y by and with the Advise and consent of this pres-

---

[1] Arch. Md., Vol., 24, p. 254.
[2] Arch. Md., Vol. 24, p. 265.

ent Generall Assembly; And by the Authority of the same that the book of Common Prayer and Administracon of the Sacraments with other Rites and Ceremonys of the Church According to the use of the Church of England; The Psalter or Psalmes of David. And Morning and Evening Prayer therein Conteyned be Sollemnly read by all and Every Minister or Reader in Every Church which now is or hereafter shall be settled and Established within this Province.

[Defines "Established Churches."]

And that all Congregations and Places for Publick Worship, according to the usage of the Church of England within this Province for the Maintenance of whose Ministers, and the persons Officiateing therein any certaine income or Revenue is or shall by the Laws of this Province be Established and Enjoyned to be raised or paid shall be deemed Settled and Established Churches;

[Tax for the "Maintenance" of Ministers.]

And for the Encouragement of Faithfull and able Ministers Labouring in the Worke of the Gospell to come and reside in this Province.

II. *Bee it Enacted* by the Authority aforesaid that a Tax or Assessm^t of Forty pound of Tob^o per Poll be Yearly and every Year Successively Levy^d upon every Taxable Person within each respective Parish within this Province. As they have been; now are or here After shall be laid out Limitted or Appointed; by Laws of this Province; And entered upon Record As the said Former Laws therein did Direct.

[Disposition of "Forty per poll" tax.]

Which said Assessment of Forty pounds of Tob° p Poll shall alwayes be Paid and Allowed to the Minister of each respective Parish haveing noe other Benefice to Officiate in; Presented; inducted or Appoynted by his Excell[cy] The Governour or Comander in Cheife for the tyme being—

[Clerk of parish church.]

And every such Minister is hereby Required and Enjoyned to Appoynt And Constantly to Keep a Clerk of Such Parish Church; and to pay and Satisfye such Clerk the Sume of One Thousand Pounds of Tob° yearly and Every year out of the Said Fourty p. poll;—

[Prevention of illegal marriages.]

And to prevent all illegall and Unlawful Marriages; not allowable by the Church of England; but forbidden by the Table of Marriages,

III. *Bee it Enacted* by the Authority aforesaid; That noe Minister, Preist or Magistrate shall Presume to joyne Together in Marriage any Person whatsoever contrary to the Table of Marriage; by this Act Appoynted to be sett up in Every Parish Church within this Province; Under the penalty of Five Thousand pounds of Tob° Nor shall any Person Forbidden to Intermarry by such Table of Marriage p'sume to be joyned in marriage Under the Like Penalty of Five Thousand pounds of Tob° such Penalty and Forfeiture; on either side; to be made to our Soveraigne Lord the King; his heires and Successors, for the uses in this Act hereafter menc̄oned;

[Who shall perform marriage ceremonies.]

And to prevent Any Lay Person From Joyning any Persons in Marriage; Where any Minister or Prest cann be had; And to Assertaine what shall be paid for Marriages.

IV. *Bee it likewise Enacted* by the Authority Aforesaid that in every Parish where any Minister or Incumbent shall reside & have Charge of Souls therein; noe Justice or Majestrate being a Lay man shall Joyne any Person in Marriage; Under the Penalty of Five Thousand Pounds of Tob° For such Offence; To our Soveraigne Lord the King; as aforesaid;—

[Marriage fees.]

And it Shall be Lawfull to every Minister; To take and receive of Every Person or Persons by him Married the Sume of Five shillings Sterling and noe more.

[Place of marriage ceremony.]

Provided such Persons come to such Parish Church or Chappell at time of Divine Service for Solemnizeing such Marriage.

[Sheriff to collect "Forty p. poll" tax.]

And for the better and more effectually collecting the said Duty of Fourty Pound of Tob° p. Poll; and paying this same to the uses by the Law intended and Appoynted.

V. *Bee it Enacted* that the Sherriffe of each Severall County shall and is hereby obliged to Collect and gather the said Assessment of Forty p. poll of the Severall persons within each respective Parish in his County; in the same mañer. And by the same authority as the Publick and County Levys are Collected;—

[To whom paid.]

and shall pay the same Forty Pounds p. Poll to the Minister or incumbent in each respective Parish;—

[Authority for vestrys.]

And the better to Promote the Execution of the good Laws of this Province; soe farr as Concerns the Respective Parishes. And for the more Easey Dispatch of Parish Business;

VI. *Bee it Further Enacted* by the Authority aforesaid, by and with the Advice and Consent aforesaid; that there be Select Vestrys, in each Parish of this Province; and that the severall Vestrymen of the Severall Parishes within this Province, That now are or hereafter shall be Chosen, be such select Vestry;—

[Number of vestrymen.]

—Of which Vestry the Number shall always be Six at least. Except upon Death or Resignation or other Discharge of any of them; according to the Provision herein made,—

[Filling vacancies in vestry.]

To that purpose and in such case of Death or Resignacon or other Legall Discharge from serveing the remaineing part of such Vestrys shall with all convenient Speed Sumon & Appoynt a Generall meeting of all the Inhabitants of the said Parish;—

[Voters must be freeholders.]

—Who are Free holders within the same Parish; and Contribute to the Public Taxes & Charges of the said Parish;—

[Vestrymen must be freeholders.]

—who shall by Majority of Voyces Collect and Choose one or more Sober and Discreet Person or persons Freeholders of each Respective Parish To supply such vacansye—

[Oath required of a vestryman.]

And such Person or Persons soe Ellected and Chosen shall take the Usuall oath appoynted by Act of Parliament instead of the Oath of Allegiance and Supremacy; and the Following Oaths viz. I doe Solemnly Swear and Declare that I will Justly and truly Execute the trust or Office of a Vestryman of this Parish. According to my best skill and Knowledge; without P^{r}judice Favor or Affec͞con;—

[Oath administered by justice of peace]

—which said Oath at the Ellec͞con of a New Vestry are to be Administered by any Justice of the Peace of the County; City or Place; where such Vestry is who is hereby required and Impowered to Administer the same.

[Additional Oaths administered by either justice of peace or the "First Vestryman."[1]]

And upon Ellec͞con Afterwards either by A Justice of Peace as aforesaid or the First Vestryman who is hereby likewise required & Impowered to Administer the same;

[Additional oaths for vestrymen.]

And each person soe Elected and Chosen; shall likewise subscribe the Test; And alsoe the *Association* and haveing soe Done, and not before shall be Deemed and taken as one of the Vestry. To all intents and purposes.

[1] Repealed May 1st, 1704, Arch. Md., Vol. 24, p. 418.

[Two new vestrymen chosen annually.]

VII. *And it is hereby further ordained and Enacted* by the Consent and Authority afores^d that Two new Vestrymen shall be Annually Chosen in the Places of Two Others who shall be Left out;

[Annual elections to be on Easter Monday.]

To wch purpose all the Inhabitants of every Parish being Freeholders within the same Parish; and Contributing to the Publick Taxes and Charges thereof, or such of them as shall think fitt to Attend; shall repair to theire respective Parish Churches, every Year Successively upon Easter Monday.

[Freeholders to name retiring vestrymen.]

And there by their Free Choyce, declare what Two Persons shall be Discharged from their being Vestrymen; And Chuse Two others Qualify'd according to this Present Act; in their stead & Room who takeing the Oaths and performing all other things required by this present Act or other the Laws of this Province for Vestrymen; Shall be Deemed and taken to be members of the said Vestry; To all intents and purposes.

[Minister to be one of the vestry.]

Provided alwayes that in every Parish where any Minister or Incumbent is or shall be Lawfully according to the Laws and usages of this Province Appointed; and in possession of any Liveing invested with the 40 p. Poll; and resideing therein he shall Dureing the continuance afors^d and noe longer, be one of the Vestry of such Parish; and Principall of such Vestry; Although there be the Number of Six persons or more beside;

[Register of parish appointed.]

And for keeping a faire Register of all such Vestrys proceedings and for Registring of all births Marriages and Burialls; in each Respective Parish.

VIII. *Bee it Enacted* by the Authority advice and consent aforesaid. That each Vestry shall and is hereby Obliged to provide a fitt Person for a Register; who shall at all times keep a true and faire Registry of the Sevāll proceeds of Such Vestry from time to time in Executeing their trust and Authority; and making just and true entrys thereof,—

[Register's oath.]

which Person soe to be Appointed for keeping such Registry, shall take the Oath substituted in the place of the Oaths of Allegiance and Supremacy and Subscribe the Test and Association; and alsoe an oath to be given him by the said Vestry; which oath the said Vestry are hereby impowered To Administer accordingly for the due and Faithfull Executeing his said Office; before he shall be Admitted into the said Office;

[Register to record vestry proceedings, etc.]

And shall make due entry of all Vestry proceedings and of all Births, Marriages and Burrials (Negroes and Mullattoes excepted) That is to say the Christian and Sir name; with the day moneth and year of every such Births, Marriages or Burryalls;

[Inhabitants of parish to furnish information.]

To which purpose all and every the Inhabitants of each Parish that are either Parent, Guardians, Overseers,

Masters or Mistresses of any person, borne Married or buried, are hereby Injoyned and required, To give Notice, to the Register of such Parish within two Moneths after such Birth, Marriage or Buriall;

[Register's fee.]

and pay him six pence for entrying it at the time of giveing Notice aforesaid

[Penalty of inhabitants for not giving information.]

—under the Penalty of one hundred pounds of Tob° To be forefeited by such Inhabitants Aforesaid; Refuseing or neglecting as aforesaid—

[Penalty of Register for refusing or neglecting to make entries.]

—under the penalty of one hundred pounds of Tob° To be forefeited by such Register refuseing or neglecting to enter it; haveing received his fee for the same.

[Register to show records of parish.]

And such Register is hereby Obliged To shew any Person or Persons Reasonably desireing it any such Register, give a Cert. of any Births, Marriages or Burialls That shall be reasonably required of him;—

[Register's fees.]

—and Shall have for Fees from such person; Six pence, for any Search, and Six pence for any Copy or Cert given as aforesaid and noe more;

[Ratifying previous parish records.]

—hereby Ratefying & confirming as Vallid all Registers, or Entrys of any Births, Marriages, or Burialls heretofore made with any Clarke of any County Court according to the direccōns of such Laws, as were then in force, before any of those Laws were in being.

[Providing record books.]

And that the Register of each Parish may be enabled to performe the Charge hereby required of him.

IX. *Bee it Enacted* by the Authority Advice and consent Aforesaid, That if there be any Vestry of any Parises that has not already Provided good and Substantiall Writeing books; well bound sufficient for registring such proceedings, in according to the direccōns of the former Laws:

[Penalty for not providing record books.]

—that in every such case of such neglect or omission the Vestry of such parish shall at the Parish charge, Provide such book or books within Six moneths from the end of this Session of Assembly under the Penalty of Five hundred pounds of Tob° each Vestryman (the minister only excepted) neglecting as aforesaid. To our Soveraigne Lord the King, for the uses within mencōned:

[Vestry meetings once a month.]

And that there may be noe neglect in the Vestry of those Employ'd under them in the Lawfull and conscionable Performance of theire Severall charges. The said Severall Vestrys are hereby obliged to meet once in every moneth, or as often as need shall require—

[Public notice of vestry meetings.]

—upon publick notice given by the Principall Vestryman of each Parish To Consult of the methods and ways of performing the severall Authorityes reposed in them.

[Penalty for absence of vestrymen.]

And from which Vestry soe Appointed, noe Vestryman being Personally summoned shall without a Lawfull or reasonable Excuse Absent himselfe under the Penalty of such Fine or Mulct as the residue of the said Vestry meeting shall Lay upon them, soe as the same never Exceeds One hundred pounds of Tob:—

[Authority to vestrymen for calling a meeting.]

—and upon default or neglect in such Principall Vestryman as is before menconed to Sumon a Vestry when there is need for one, and he is thereunto requested any other Three of the Vestry or if there shall happen by any Accident To be but Two of the said Vestry, beside the Principall Vestryman resideing in the said Parish, such Three or Two shall have power and Authority To Sumon and Appoint a Vestry to be holden:—

[Record of vestry proceedings to be kept in register.]

And all such omission and neglects to be noted in the Vestrys Reg^r of proceedings And any forfeiture thereby incur'd to be recovered in his Majesty's name—

[Table of marriages to be provided.]

—and the said severall and respective Vestrys are hereby further Enjoyned That where there is not Tables of Marriages already put up in theire respective Parish

Churches, with all convenient Speed, and within Six moneths at the most To procure a faire Table of Marriages Transcribed and sett up In theire respective Churches and the same keep continually in theire said Churches and persons being thereby informed what Marriages are forbidden may avoyd the Contracting of any such unlawfull marriages.

[Church wardens appointed each year.]

And that the said Vestrymen & the rest of the Inhabitants of every Parish being free holders within the same Parish and contributeing to the Publick Taxes and charges there doe once every year upon Easter Munday yearly make Choyce and Appoint Two sober and Discreet Persons freeholders of their respective Parishes: To be Church Wardens for that year.

[All freeholders of parish vote on church wardens.]

All the Inhabitants of every Parish, being freeholders within the same Parish and contributing to the Publick Taxes and charges thereof. Have in Liberty alsoe To vote in the Choyce of Church wardens.—

[Penalty of vestrymen for nonperformance of duty.]

—each Vestryman Expecting as before Excepted being under the Penalty of Two hundred pounds of Tob° for neglecting either to procure a Table of Marriages or to Appoynt Church Wardens; To our Soveraigne Lord the King as aforesaid,—

[Oath of church wardens.]

—which Church Wardens soe Chosen shall Take the usuall Oaths. And likewise declare on his Oath to be

Administered unto him by the Vestry to whome power is hereby given. To Administer the same Accordingly: well and Faithfully to Execute that Office for the Ensueing year: According to the Lawes and Usages of the said Province to the best of his Skill and power and untill he shall be thereof duly Discharged.

[Fines for church wardens.]

And any such person or persons soe Chosen Church Warden or Wardens; that shall wilfully refuse To Serve in the said Office and take the Oaths aforesaid: shall be find one thousand pounds of Tob° To our Soveraigne Lord the King:—

[Church wardens and vestry to see that parochial charges are paid.]

And the Church Wardens and Vestry are Authorized and required To take constant care To satisfye and pay the Parochiall charges and all necessary repaires and Amendm^{ts} of theire respective Churches, Chappels or Church yards, and cause the same at all time to be repaired and Amended as need shall require:—

[To be paid out of gifts to the parish.]

—out of such gifts, goods or Chattels, as shall come to their hands for the Church or Parish use: and the payment of with Parochiall charges.

[Fines to be levied by church wardens.]

All the Fines forefeitures and Mulcts, by this Law incurr'd shall be Levyed by the Church Wardens in each respective Parish. And by them accordingly Applyed;

and in Case they shall not have sufficient Effects to pay Parochiall charges as aforesaid or to make such necessary repaires as is required:—

[Justices of county courts to assess ten pounds of tobacco.]

Then and not otherwise it shall be Lawfull for the Justices of the County Courts upon Applycacon of such parish Vestry and Church Wardens, To Assess the respective parishes by a certaine sume of Tob° not exceeding Tenn pounds of Tob° by the Poll in any one year:—

[Sheriff authorized to collect tax.]

—which Assessm^t made by such County Court: And a Certificate thereof under the County Seale shall be sufficient to the Sherriff of such County to Levy such Tax by the Poll on the Taxables of such Parishes in the same mañer as other Public dues are Levyed—

[Sheriff's fees.]

—and shall not deduct above Five p. hundred for his Sallery,—

[Church maintenance tax paid to vestry.]

—and pay the same to such Vestry for the use aforesaid.

[Defines the purposes of this Act.]

And to the intent that this Act may Answer the end of the makers, which is that his Ma^{tyes} Good Subjects of this Province may be instructed in Religion and therein of their Duty to God, his Ma^{tye} and themselves, And those pious and Exemplary persons that shall Labour therein Suitably provided for—

[Ministers limited to two parishes.]

X. *Bee it Enacted* by the Authority Advice and consent aforesaid, that no Minister or Incumbent shall at one time hold more than two parishes—

[Minister's hold two charges subject to vestrys of the two parishes.]

—nor Two [parishes] unless by the desire or Agreement of the Vestry of the said Adjacent parish and consent of the Vestryes where he resides. And appoyntment of the Ordinary,

[Lay Readers appointed by vestry and licensed by the Ordinary.]

—and where there are not or shall not be Ministers in any Parish it shall and may be Lawfull to the Vestry To provide some Sober and Discreet person as a Reader, And present him to the Ordinary,—

[Lay reader's Salary.]

—who may Sequester part of the Forty pounds p. poll; To pay him for such Service;

[Remainder of "Forty p. poll".]

And the rest to be Apply'd as the Law in cases of such Vacancies directs.

[Lay Readers' oaths and license.]

And upon such Readers takeing the Aforesaid Oathes Appoynted by Act of Parliament; Subscribing the Test and Association, and procureing Lycence from the Ordinary—

[Lay Reader's duty.]

—shall and may read Divine Service, Homilies and such other good Authors of Practicall Divinity as shall be Appointed: at the usuall Times in such Churches or Chapp^{lls} and therein shall Demean himself according to the Lyturgy of the Church of England as aforesaid:—

[Vestry meetings dates fixed.]

And for the Preventing of Delayes and other inconveniences which might happen if there were a necessity for the Expecting the Attendance and presence of all the said Vestrymen; And at the same time to prevent the doeing of any thing of Consequence by Surprize by a small number of them.—

XI. *Bee it hereby Enacted*, That the First Tuesday in Every Moneth shall be and is hereby fixt and Ascertained for holding a Vestry at a Eleven of the Clock in the Forenoon in the usuall place for that purpose, without any notice or warning to be given thereof,—

[Number constituting a vestry meeting.]

—at which time and Place, the major part of the Vestrymen then present (soe as such Majority be not under the number of Three persons) shall be esteemed a Vestry.

[Authority for vestry to act.]

And shall have full power to ord^r Direct and Act in all things, by this Act Appoynted. To be done According to this Act as a Vestry;—

[Vestryman to be removed for non attendance.]

And that in case any Vestryman shall remove or with draw himselfe from the Parish or Voluntarily or Freequently neglect to give his Attendance, and Absent himselfe from the Vestry or otherwayes become unfitt or Incapable to continue To execute the said Office or Trust, that in any such case the residue of the said Vestry or the majority of them (soe as such majority be not under the number of Three persons) shall and may have power After personall Notice given to such party if it conveniently may be, or the affixing of a publick notice upon the great Door of the Church for three Severall Sundays Successively. If personall notice can not be given without great Difficulty charge or Delay, of their Intentions to proceed in such manner To remove such person from being a Vestryman and to declare his Office voyd—

[Electing new vestrymen in usual way.]

—to Sum̃on a meeting of the Parishioners Qualified as is above Directed for the Electing another in the place of such person (who shall after Allowing a reasonable time to such person to make his complaint if he Apprehend himselfe injuryed not exceeding a Fortnight) Proceed to a new Election accordingly—

[Register must show vestry books and parish accounts.]

And that there may not be any appression^t or misapplycacon of the publick Revenue by such Vestrys or just cause of Complaint Against them in any of theire proceedings without redress.

XII. *Bee it Enacted* by the Authority advice and consent aforesaid, that all and every Parishioner and Parishioners whatsoever who contribute to the Publick Taxes and charges of the said Parish shall and may require the Register herein before mencōned. At any reasonable or Convenient time or Times to give them an Inspection of the Vestry books and Accompts of all every theire orders and proceedings.

[Register to make copy of records.]

And shall and may take Copy thereof paying a reasonable Fee for the same according to the length thereof, and the trouble of Attendance.

[Appeals from parish records to be made to the Governour or Deputy Governour and Councill.]

And that all and every Person and persons whatsoever who shall find or Apprehend him her or themselves grieved or Injuried, or that the body of the Parish is injuried or Appressed by any Acts, Orders, Rules, Accounts or other proceedings of any such Vestry. The partyes soe injuryed or any other in their behalfe or in right of the whole body may from time to time Appeale for Redress against all and every such orders Accounts and other proceedings. To the Governour or Deputy Governour for the time being, and Councill of the said Province,—

[Decision of Governour and Council to be final.]

—who are hereby required and impowered to Examine, hear and Determine, all and every such Appeale and Complaints for Redress. And to give Redress as they in theire Judgm^t shall think agreeable to Justice and Equity; and such their order Judgm^t and Decree; shall be finall & bind all parties; the right of Appeal being alwayes Reserved to his Ma^tye in Councill according to the Lawes of this Province—

[Exemption of dissenters and Quakers.]

Provided alwayes that every of his Ma^tyes Protestant Subjects within this Province; Decenting from the Church of England. As to matters relateing to the Worshipp and Service of Almighty God And the Decenters Comonly called Quakers in all matters relateing To the takeing of Oathes and all protestant Decenters whatsoever as to all discharges and Exemplicacon from penaltyes or forfeitures upon Acc^t of theire Desenting Separate meetings or other matters wherein Tolleracon and ease is granted. To Protestant Decenters by one Act made in the First Year of the reigne of his present Ma^tye and his late Consort Queen Mary of Blessed Memory Entituled An Act for Exempting theire Ma^tyes Protestant Subjects Decenting from the Church of England from the Penaltyes of Cert Lawes; And by another Act made in the 7th and 8th years of the Reigne of his present Ma^tye Intituled An Act that the Solemn Affirmacon or Declar of the people called Quakers shall be Accepted instead of an oath in the Usual forme, Shall have the full benefitt of all Exemptions ease and Indulgence by the said Acts granted and allowed according to the True intent and meaning of the s^d Acts they respectively confirming themselves in theire meeting and Assembling.

[Jurisdiction of local Justices of Peace.]

And all other things to the ord^r and rules Enjoined by the said Acts with this Alteracon only that the severall things required or appointed by the s^d Acts to be done by or at the Gen^ll or Quarter Session of the Peace or any other Court whatsoever or by Two or to any one single Justice of the Peace shall be done by to and at the respective County Courts of this Province within whose Jurisdiction the matter shall fall out; and before to or by the Justices of the same.

[Dissenters' places of worship to be registered.]

And that the severall places used for Religious worsh^pp by any such Decenting Congregacon or Assembly shall be Certified unto and Register'd at the s^d County Court, in the same mañer, as is by the said first mencond Act appointed to be done, To the Bishop of the Diocesse, The Arch Deacon of the Arch Deaconary, and the Justices of the Peace At theire generall or Quarter Sessions.

[Repeal of Act of 1700.]

Provided alsoe and

XIII. *Be it further Enacted*, that one Act made at a Gen^ll Assembly, begun and held at the Port of Annapolis the 26th day of Aprill 1700 Intituled an Act for the Service of Almighty God, and Establishm^t of Religion in this Province According to the Church of England, &c Bee and is hereby repealed and made voyd."

"The Governor endorsed the bill in these words vizt 'On behalfe of his most Sacred Maj^tye King William the Third &c I will these to be Laws'

N. Blakiston"[1]

March 25th, 1702.[2]

[1] Arch. Md., Vol. 24, p. 264.
[2] It is apparent that the news of the death of King William which occurred on the 8th of March had not reached the Province of Maryland at the time this bill was passed.

"Which being done his Ex^cy was pleased to Seale them with the Broad Seale of this Province............, Thereupon M^r. Speaker and the rest of the Members were prorogued (until 25th of April) accordingly.

Soe ended the Second Sessions of the Assembly on Wednesday the 25th day of March Anno Dni. 1702 and in the 14th yeare of the Reigne of our Sovereigne Lord William the third by the Grace of God of Engl^d Scotl^d France and Ireland King defender of the faith, &c.

W. Taylard,
Clk: house Dell."[1]

---

[1] Arch. Md., Vol. 24, p. 264.

VALIDITY OF THE ACT OF 1702

"At the Court of St James[1]
18th January 1702/3

Present the Queen's Maj^{tie} in Councell

Whereas—By Powers granted under the Great Seal of England, the Governor, Council and Assembly of her Maj^{ties} Province of Maryland have been authorized and impowered to constitute and ordaine Laws, Statutes and Ordinaries which are to be in force until her Maj^{ties} pleasure shall be signified to the Contrary, and

Whereas—Pursuant to the said powers an Act has been lately passed by the Governor, Council and Assembly of the said Province entitled 'An Act for the Establishment of Religious Worship in this Province according to the Church of England and for the Maintenance of Ministers' which said Act having, upon the perusal of the Lords Com^{rs} of Trade and Plantation been p^{r}scribed by her Maj^{tie} for her approbation of this Board.

Her Maj^{tie} with the advice of her Governor and Council is pleased to declare her approbation of the same.

Pursuant to her Maj^{ties} pleasure herein signified, the said Law is hereby confirmed and finally enacted and ratified accordingly.

John Povey"
[Deputy Secretary of the Plantation Office]

---

[1] Vestry Proceedings, All Saints Parish, Calvert County.

"Maryland s s

> By the Honorable Presid^{nt} & Councell
>
> 22nd June 1703
>
> Ordered that her Maj^{ties} most Sacred Maj^{ties} Royall Assent to the Act of Religion (as above) be published by the severall Minist^r at the parish Churches the First Tuesday in August.
>
> > Signed p order
> > Wm Bladen
> > Clk Council.
>
> At A Vestry Meeting
>
> 3rd August 1703
>
> This day according to the Order of the President and Council was published her Maj^{ties} Royall Assent to the Act of Religion. The vestry being present. Mr Thos. Cockshutt, Mr Wm Dalrumple, Mr James Heigh, M^r Ed$^{w.}$ Baleter and Mr Joseph Hall."[1]

---

[1] Vestry Proceedings, All Saints Parish, Calvert County.

BASIS OF CLAIM THAT THIS ACT WAS VOID

"The following facts may be premised as the case—King William deceased on the 8th of March 1701/2; the assembly, which was therefore called in the usual manner met on the 16th of the same month, and during its sitting passed the Act in question, without the possibility of knowing, that such an event had taken place. Governor Seymour the successor of Governor Blackistone, who summoned the assembly upon his arrival, on the 11th of April, 1704, found the same assembly existing, that had been called, by his predecessor, in the name of King William; so that there were three several seccessions of assembly held, after the demise of King William, to wit, in June 1702, in October 1703, and in April 1704."[1]

"The Act of 1701/2 under which the claim was preferred was passed by a House of Delegates chosen under writs of election issued the name of King William, the Government [of Maryland] being then in the hands of the Crown. A few days after the decease of this King and without any fresh writs of election or summons, the Assembly was convened and the Act in question was passed. It was now [1772] contended that by the death of the king that Assembly was dissolved; and that this Act being passed thereafter, was absolutely void, and not susceptible of confirmation by subsequent acts merely presuming its existence.

The opinions of Mr. Hollyday and Mr. Dulany, sustaining the validity of the Act; and those of Mr. Paca and Mr. Chase in opposition to it, have been preserved and are remarkable for their ingenious views and profound investigations."[2]

The American Revolution settled the controversy over the validity of the Act of 1702 before it reached the courts.

[1] Chalmers, Opinions of Eminent Lawyers, p. 303.
[2] McMahon, History of Maryland, p. 399.

DISPOSITION OF "FORTY PER POLL."

"At a Council held at the Port of Annapolis
Friday, March 20th 1702.

Present

His Excellency the Governour, (Nathaniel Blackiston)

Col. John Addison
Thomas Brooke, Esqr
Col. John Courts

Col. Edwd Lloyd
Lt. Col. Wm Holland
James Saunders Esqr

And this Board being of opinion that all Tob° raised by the 40 lb p. Poll whilst no incumbent in the Parish and lodged in the Vestry's Hands *is not the right of any minister* who are only by law entituled to that part of the 40 lb. p. Poll proportionable to such Time they shall officiate in their respective Parishes, and that such Tob° ought to be applyed by the Vestry for the use of the Parish."[1]

---

[1] Arch. Md., Vol. 24, p. 217.

DISPOSITION OF TOBACCO TAX[1]
Repair Churches, Buy Land, Stock for Glebes, etc.
Act of 1704

Title.
"An Act to Declare how the forty pounds of Tobacco p. poll in such Parishes where there is no Incumbent shall be disposed of.

[Preamble.]
Whereas by an Act of Assembly made at a Generall Assembly begun and held at the Port of Annapolis the twenty sixth day of April One thousand Seven hundred and two Entituled an Act for the Service of Allmighty God and Establishment of Religion in this Province according to the Church of England, &c* There is no provision made where there is a Vacancy or no Incumbent in a Parish how or to what use the forty pounds of tobacco p. Poll shall be Applyed.

Therefore the Burgesses and Delegates of this present Generall Assembly pray that it may be Enacted and—

[Vestrymen to have control.]

I. *Be it Enacted* by the Queens most excellent Majesty by and with the advice and Consent of her Majesty's Governour Councill and Assembly of this Province and the authority of the same. That what tobacco of the s^d forty p. poll hath, is or shall become due in any Parish where there is hath or shall be no incumbent the said tobacco shall be Employed and applyed to and for the uses following (that is to say) by the Vestrymen of each respective Parish—

[1] Arch. Md., Vol. 24, p. 420.

[Vestrymen to use it for repairing Churches, etc.]

—who are hereby Empowered to dispose thereof for and toward the repairing such Churches as are allready built finishing and Compleating the insides thereof as the said Vestrymen shall think fitt or for the purchasing a Pulpit Cloth Cushion bible or Common Prayer book or Church Plate for the use of the said Church

[Confirming Vestry's Action.]

And of any Vestry hath already applyed or laid out the said Tobacco or any part thereof to the uses aforesaid such application or disposals is hereby Confirmed.

[To build new Churches.]

II. *And be it further Enacted* by the Authority aforesaid by and with the Advice and Consent af^d that in Any Parish where the Church is old or so out of repair as not fitt to be made use of and shall be so adjudged by the Vestrymen of such Parish It shall and may be Lawfull to and for such Vestrymen to apply the said forty pounds of tobacco p. poll for the building of a new one—

[Empower the Vestrymen to buy land.]

And it hath or shall so happen by reason of a Long Vacancy in such Parish that there shall be no occassion to apply the said Tobacco to the uses afd or of any such tobacco after such application hath or shall remaine in the hands of the Vestry The Vestry s^d are hereby directed and Empowered to purchase therewith either a plantation with a Tract of Land or a Certaine Tract of Land as near and contiguous to the Churche belonging to such Parishes as may be (and if there be no Church in such Parishes then to purchase a tract of Land as may be most Convenient for the Inhabitants thereof and build a Church thereon)

[Property to be known as Glebe.]

Which Plantation or Land shall be and forever remaine as a Glebe to the use of the ministers of such Parish for the time being who shall be Lawfully inducted and appointed according to the usage of the Church of England and this Province.

[Surplus Tobacco to be used for "Stocking" the Glebe.]

And if there shall happen in any Parish to be Tobacco over and above answering the uses aforesaid it shall be Employed to the Improvement and Stocking such Glebe as the Vestry Shall Judge most Proper.

[Sheriffs fees for collecting the "forty p. poll."]

And forasmuch as by the said recited act there is nothing Allowed to the Sheriffe for Collecting the said forty pounds of Tobacco p. poll and paying the same to the incumbent or Vestry—

III. *Bee it Enacted* by the Authority af[d] that the Sheriffs of each respective County shall have allowed him or them, out of the said forty pounds of tobacco per poll which they shall pay to such Vestry or incumbent, five pounds of Tobacco p. cent for Collecting and Paying the same and no more, any Law Statute or usage to the Contrary notwithstanding.

May the 2[d] 1704
Read and Assented to by
the house of Delegates
    W. Taylard
        Clk House Del.

May the 2[d] 1704
Read and Assented to by
her Maj[ties] hon[ble] Councill
    W. Bladen
        Cl. Council.

May the third Seventeen hundred and four

On behalf of her most sacred Majesty Anne by the Grace of God of England Scotland France and Ireland and the Dominions thereunto belonging Queen Defender of the faith, &c^a

I will this to be a law.

      Jo. Seymour   { 'with the Great Seal of Maryland Sealed.'" }

PART VI.

COUNTIES, PARISHES, HUNDREDS, CHURCHES VESTRYMEN AND MINISTERS, ETC.

PARISHES

"In England the parish may be regarded as essentially an Ecclesiastical institution being defined as the township or cluster of towns which was assigned to the ministration of a single priest, etc.

The beginnings of the parochial system are attributed to Theodore of Tarsus who was Archbishop of Canterbury toward the close of the seventh century . . . . The two systems, the parish and the township, have existed for more than a thousand years side by side, identical in area and administered by the same persons and yet separate in character and machinery.

The boundaries of the old ecclesiastical parishes are usually identical with those of the township or townships comprised within its precinct . . . . many parishes contain more than one township."[1]

HUNDREDS

The work of dividing the counties into parishes by the Justices and Freeholders showed that they followed the lines of the hundreds or districts of the counties. According to Webster's Dictionary a "hundred" is a division of a county supposed to contain a hundred families.

"The origin of these divisions (lathe, soke, tithing, hundreds, etc.) is generally ascribed to the creative genius of Alfred [The Great, 849–901] who, according to the popular theory, divided the country into counties, the county into hundreds, and the hundreds into tithings, or towns."[2]

[1] Encycl. Brit., Vol. 18, p. 295 (9th Ed.).
[2] Encycl. Brit., Vol. 12, p. 360 (9th Ed.).

CHURCHES STANDING BEFORE THE ESTABLISHMENT

"Before 1691 there were the following Churches[1]

County	Church	Minister
St. Mary's	Trinity	Rev. Mr. Davis
do	St. George's	do
do	St. Paul's	do
Charles	Christ	Rev. Mr. Moore
do	Portobacco	do
Calvert	Christ	Rev. Mr. Turling
do	All Faith's	do
do	St. Paul's	do
Baltimore	St. George's	....
do	St. John's	....
Cecil	North Sassafras	Rev. Mr. Vanderbush
.do	South Sassafras	do
Kent	Kent Island	....
do	St. Paul's	....
Talbot	St. Luke's	Rev. Mr. Lillingston
do	St. Paul's	do
do	Wye	Revs. Clayland and Leach
Dorchester	Dorchester [Trinity]	Rev. Mr. Huett
Somerset	All Saints Monii	Rev. Mr. Huett
Anne Arundel	Herring Creek	....
do	All Hallows	....

[1] From the manuscript of the late Dr. Ethan Allen, Protestant Episcopal clergyman, for many years Historiographer of the Diocese of Maryland, Photostat Copy, p. 15.

PROPOSED SEAL FOR THE COUNTIES OF THE PROVINCE OF MARYLAND
Authorized 1692. Arch. Md., Vol. 13, f. 290 and Vol. 8, f. 383. It is not now known that any of these seals were made.

COUNTIES OF MARYLAND—1692[1]

The Provincial Assembly resolved after debate that the members from the Counties take "precedency"[2] as follows:

"City of St Maryes
1. St Maryes County
2. Kent   "
3. Ann Arundall   "
4. Calvart   "
5. Charles   "
6. Baltemore County
7. Talbott   "
8. Sumersett   " ·
9. Dorchester   "
10. Cecill   " "

There were protests made against this order by the residents of Kent County. They wanted to be recognized as the oldest county of the Province. Among other protests one was presented to the Assembly on Oct. 15th, 1695, and Mr. Matthew Erexon (Eareckson), an inhabitant of the "Isle of Kent" was allowed to speak on its merits.[3] The official recognition of this petition and the ruling of the Council appears as follows:

"Council Chamber May 2^d 1696[4]

Kent Island petition produced and Ordered sent down [to the Lower House] with the following endorsement, vizt—

By His Excell'ncy the Gov^{nr} and Council &c. Upon reading the within Petition it was Ordered that the same be sent down but with this note that His Excell^{cy} will in no wise Assent to any Alteration contrary to the late Act and that whereas it is insisted upon that they [the Inhabitants of the Isle of Kent] are the most antient County, it is Observed that the first People that Inhabited the same did not acknowledge themselves Belonging to this Province and therefore are not the most antient County."

[1] The arrangement of the counties is in accordance with the date of their erection. Under this plan the parishes are given numbers in accordance with those of the county in which they were erected.
[2] Arch. Md., Vol. 13, p. 350.
[3] Arch. Md., Vol. 19, p. 251.
[4] Arch. Md., Vol. 19, p. 300.

THE PARISHES ERECTED IN 1692-1693

County	Parish
1. St. Mary's	1. William and Mary
	2. King and Queen
2. Kent	3. Kent Island or Christ Church
	4. St. Paul's
3. Anne Arundel	5. Herring Creek or St. James
	6. South River or All Hallows
	7. Middle Neck or St. Ann's
	8. Broad Neck or Westminster
4. Calvert	9. Christ Church
	10. All Saints
	11. St. Paul's
	12. All Faiths
5. Charles	13. William and Mary or Pickawaxon
	14. Port Tobacco
	15. Nanjemy or Durham
	16. Piscataway or St. John's
6. Baltimore	17. Patapsco or St. Paul's
	18. St. John's or Copley
	19. St. George's
7. Talbot	20. St. Paul's
	21. St. Peter's
	22. St. Michael's
8. Somerset	23. Somerset
	24. Coventry
	25. Stepney
	26. Snow Hill or All Hallows
9. Dorchester	27. Great Choptank
	28. Dorchester
10. Cecil	29. So. Sassafrax or Shrewsbury
	30. No. Sassafrax or St. Stephen's

I have not been able to find a record of St. Andrew's Parish having been laid out in 1692 though the Fulham papers are said to mention it as one of the original parishes of the Province of Maryland. In 1744 a St. Andrew's Parish was erected in St. Mary's County. It would seem probable that it would have been erected in Cecil County had all of the territory of that County been taken into consideration. North Sassafras Parish, in Cecil County, apparently did not cover all of the part of the county which lay north of the Sassafras River at that time, 1692.

ST. MARY'S COUNTY

Named in honor of the Blessed Virgin Mary, the landing in St. Mary's of the Colonists having been made on the Feast of the Annunciation, March 25th, 1634.

ST. MARY'S COUNTY (erected 1637) bounds began at Point Lookout thence with the Potomac river to the southern boundary of Charles County, then in an easterly direction to a line paralleling the "Three Notched Road," then the line ran to Pyne Hill creek or river, then down this creek to the Chesapeake bay and thence to the place of beginning. It will be observed that St. Mary's county did not extend to the Patuxent river; the "Three Notched Road" practically divided it from Calvert county on the north.

No. 1

Shortly after the "Establishment" the lines were changed (1695), and are described in the Assembly records[1] as follows: "St. Mary's county Bounds begin on the lower side of Birds [now Budd's] creek on the Potomock river and so runne to the lower side of Indian creek on Potuxent river—, and that the divisions be straight lines from the heads of the said creekes."

"S⁽ᵗ⁾ MARIES COUNTY is divided into Ten Hundreds besides the City, viz⁽ᵗ⁾—

Resurrection
S⁽ᵗ⁾ Maries
New Town
Choptico
S⁽ᵗ⁾ Michaells
St. Georges

[1] Arch. Md., Vol. 23, p. 23.

TRINITY
ST. MARY'S CITY, ST. MARY'S COUNTY
Built of brick from the Old State House.

ST. ANDREW

LEONARDTOWN, ST. MARY'S COUNTY

St Inego's
St Clements
Harvy
   and
Poplar Hill   }
St Maries City."[1]

"St MARIES COUNTY COURT to be kept in St Maries City and that the State House there be for a Court house and Church the Act to take place on the 23^d of April next [1695] being St Georges day."[2]

"St MARIES COUNTY is divided into two Parishes, and that the same be divided between New Town hundred and Clements hundred by Mr Langworths Branch [now St. Clements river] which leads to the Petuxant main road and the s^d branch divides the said hundreds & parishes the Lower whereof being called by the Name of William and Mary Parish and the Upper by the Name of King and Queen Parish."[3]

"It was by the Justices and Freeholders of the said county—met at New Town the day and year above said—5th day of September 1692."

IN THE REPORT to the Assembly in 1694, July 30th, we find the following:—

"SAINT MARIES COUNTY is divided into two parishes which both contain about One thousand Tythables.
   1 Church built at St Georges.
   1 Church to be built near Capt Cood's.
No minister inducted.
A Glebe at St. Georges of 300 Acres Rented at 2000 ^{lbs} of tobacco per Annum."[4]

[1] Arch. Md., Vol. 23, p. 17.
[2] Arch. Md., Vol. 19, p. 159.
[3] Arch. Md., Vol. 23, p. 17.
[4] Arch. Md., Vol. 20, p. 106.

WILLIAM AND MARY PARISH embraced all that part of St. Mary's County lying between St. Clement's bay and Point Lookout on the Chesapeake bay. Its boundaries were "the Potomac river, St. Clement's bay and river, the Calvert County boundary line. [then near the Three Notched road] to Pine Hill creek and with Pine Hill creek to the Chesapeake, thence down the Chesapeake bay to Point Lookout."[1]

No, 1

"VESTRYMEN for William and Mary Parish chosen, &^{ca} vizt
Mr Kenelm Cheseldyne
Maj. John Campbell
Mr Robert Mason
Mr John Watson
Mr John Llewellin
Mr Thomas Beale"[2]

THE FIRST CHURCH in this parish was St. George's Church built, about 1642, at Poplar Hill.[3] It was the second Protestant church built in the Province.
MR. THOMAS DAVIES was lay reader in 1691.[4] Mr. ――――― Crawford officiated in 1694,[5] no minister having been inducted. The Rev. Benjamin Nobbes was rector from 1696 to 1700.[6]

---

[1] Chronicles of Colonial Maryland, p. 204.
[2] Arch. Md., Vol. 23, p. 17.
[3] Chronicles of Colonial Maryland, p. 205.
[4] Allen Ms., p. 15.
[5] Arch. Md., Vol. 20, p. 106.
[6] B. C. Steiner, Md. Hist. Mag., Vol. 12, p. 118.

ST. GEORGE

POPLAR HILL, ST. MARY'S COUNTY

It was here that the first permanent Church of England Clergyman, the Rev. William Wilkinson, M.A. (Oxon.), began in 1650 his 13 years of ministry in the Province.

CHRIST, BUILT 1737
CHAPTICO, ST. MARY'S COUNTY

This church succeeds the one built in 1642 by Thomas Gerrard. He presented the congregation that same year with a glebe.

THE FIRST PARISHES OF THE PROVINCE OF MARYLAND 113

KING AND QUEEN PARISH extended from St. Clements bay and river to the extreme end of St. Mary's county as then defined and which embraced within its limits the territory known as Newport Hundred, now part of Charles County.
No. 2

Its boundaries were St. Clements bay and "run" [then known as "Mr. Langworth's Branch"], the Calvert County line [near the "Three Notched Road"] to the upper extremity of Newport Hundred, thence to the headwaters of Wicomico river [now Zachia's swamp] and with the Wicomico river and the Potomac river to the beginning.

"VESTRYMEN for King & Queen Parish Chosen & ᶜᵃ Viz^t—

Col. Nehemiah Blackiston
Capt John Cood
Mr Richard Clouds
Capt John Dent
Mr Philip Brisco
Mr Jno Barecraft.[1]

THE FIRST CHURCH was probably "Newport Church" then located west of the center of the parish near Newport. The Episcopal Church of St. Clements manor on St. Pauls' creek, erected in 1642, was the third Protestant church built by the Colonists. A Chapel built prior to 1692 on Church "run," stood at Wicomico between Plowden's Wharf and Bluff Point.[2] "The church for King & Queen parish in St. Mary's County is built at Wicomico on land belonging 1696 to Capt. Gerrard Slye."[3]

"REV. MR. THOS. DAVIS minister prior to 1691."[4]
The Rev. Christopher Platts was rector of this parish in 1696–1700.[5]

[1] Arch. Md., Vol. 23, p. 18.
[2] Chronicles of Colonial Maryland, Thomas.
[3] Arch. Md., Vol. 20, p. 585, and Md. Cal. of Wills, Vol. 1, p. 48.
[4] Allen Ms. p. 15
[5] B. C. Steiner, Md. Hist. Magazine, Vol. 12, p. 118.

KENT COUNTY
Named for the English county of Kent.

KENT COUNTY'S (erected 1642) boundaries went through many changes prior to the "Establishment" and it may prove of interest to state here the most important ones.

No. 2

The Isle of Kent had once comprised the whole of the Eastern Shore of the Province north of the Choptank river and in his "History of Maryland" McMahon says "The subdivision called the Isle of Kent being in its origin, as was St. Mary's, the name of an undefined settlement, the County of Kent received its definite limits from the erection of other counties around it."[1]

The County of Kent comprised at successive times parts of Baltimore and Cecil counties and received its present limits or bounds in 1706. The boundaries in 1692 of Kent county comprised the whole of Kent Island and that portion of the present county that lies south of a line that ran from "Buck Neck," at the head of Worton creek, to some point on Morgan's creek.

The land records of Baltimore county prior to the erection (in 1674) of Cecil county indicate that the southern bounds of Baltimore county were as stated in the above paragraph.

Kent's boundaries became confused by the proclamation erecting Cecil county, and protests from the inhabitants of the lower part of Kent county brought forth another proclamation as follows: "Forasmuch as by a late Proclamation bearing date the sixth day of this instant June some Additions were made to several counties upon the division of that of Baltimore County and by the proclamation it was then declared that Swan Point downe to Hell point on

[1] McMahon, Hist. of Md., p. 82.

EMMANUEL
Chestertown, Kent County

It was upon the site of this church that stood the one in which it was moved and adopted, by the Convention in 1780, that "the Church of England as heretofore so known in the Province of Maryland be now called the Protestant Episcopal Church." This was the initial adoption of the name, the other dioceses following in close order. A Chapel of Ease of St. Paul's Parish in Kent County was built in Chestertown prior to 1709 and in 1721 a more substantial edifice replaced the old wooden one. In 1765 Chester Parish was laid out and then the Chapel of Ease at Chestertown became the Chapel of Ease of Chester Parish, the parish Church being built at the Cross Roads called I. U. In 1770 the Chapel of Ease at

VESTRY HOUSE, BUILT 1766
St. Paul's Parish, Kent County

One of two such buildings erected in original parishes in the Province. The other one is in St. George's Parish, Harford County.

Chester River should be and remaine for the future belonging to that Eastern side of the Bay lately erected and called by the name of Cecill County upon further consideration hereof it is thought most necessary that so much of the Eastern side as was formerly added to Kent County doe still remaine and belong to the said County as afore notwithstanding that part of the said proclamation, in witness whereof I have hereunto set my hand and caused the lesser seale of this Province to be hereunto affixed the 19th day of June in the 42nd Yeare of the Dominion of Cecilius, &c. Annoq Dmi 1674

"To all whom these may Concern"[1]

"KENT COUNTY is divided into Seven Hundreds vizt—
 Town Hundred   Island Hundred
 Chester River Lower "   Eastern Neck "
 Langfords Bay " "   Chester Upper "
 Swann Creek "   "[2]

"KENT COUNTY has 2 parishes
 1 Church built (Kent Island)
 another laid out to be built; but noe minister"[3]

Report to Assembly July 30th, 1694.

"KENT COUNTY is divided into two parishes vizt— Kent Island & St Paul's Parish. Kent Island Parish is bounded Natureally within its Self. St Paul's Parish consists of the Rest of the County."[4]

THE COURT FOR KENT was held in the house of the prominent freeholders until 1680 at which time a Court House was built in the town of New Yarmouth on Gray's Inn Creek. In 1696 it was abandoned and a Court House built on the present site at Chestertown.[5]

[1] Arch. Md., Vol. 15, p. 41. (Signed by Charles Calvert.)
[2] Arch. Md., Vol. 23, p. 25.
[3] Arch. Md., Vol. 20, p. 107.
[4] Arch. Md., Vol. 23, p. 21.
[5] Arch. Md., Vol. 19, p. 376.

No. 3

"KENT ISLAND PARISH is bounded Natureally within it Self."[1] The Chesapeake bay and the Chester river washed its northern and western shores. Eastern bay and the "Narrows" divided it from the main land on the east and south. This parish was also known as Christ Church Parish in 1698.[2]

"VESTRYMEN for the s^d Parish Chosen &^{ca} vizt
 Mr John Coppage
 Coll. Wm Laurence
 Mr Philip Conner
 Mr Alexander Walkers
 Mr Edward James
 Mr Valentine Southern"[3]

BROAD CREEK CHURCH was erected on Kent Island in 1652 according to the various authorities who have written of this island parish. The old site is at the head of Broad creek and it is said that the water in the creek was deep enough at the time the church was built to allow boats to land at its doors. It is near the place supposed to have been selected by Cleyborn for the holding of divine services when "he brought the Rev. Mr. Richard James to the Island in 1631."[4]

Anthony Workman[5] left £50 on Sept. 6th, 1708, "for erecting a Church in Christ Church Parish, Kent."

---

[1] Arch. Md., Vol. 23, p. 21.
[2] Maryland Calendar Wills, Vol. 3, p. 21.
[3] Arch. Md., Vol. 23, p. 21.
[4] Claiborne and Kent Island in Maryland History by DeCoursey W. Thom.
[5] Md. Calendar of Wills, Vol. 1, p. 115.

CHRIST
STEVENSVILLE, KENT ISLAND

This is the successor of the church that was built on Broad Creek about 1652, the ruins of which are about one mile south of Stevensville. Twenty-one years prior to the building of the old church the Reverend Richard James had preached to the settlers on the "Isle of Kent."

ST. PAUL, BUILT 1713

St. Paul's Parish, Kent County

This old church enjoys the distinction of being the oldest building in Maryland which has been in use as a place of worship continuously. It is the third church built within the present bounds of St. Paul's Parish. The first one was called St. Peter's and built on Church Creek about 1652.

ST. PAUL'S PARISH "consists of the rest of the County."[1]
No. 4
The Chesapeake bay from Worton creek south to the Chester river bounded the parish on the west, the Chester river also bounded it on the south and east. The northern line ran from Morgan's creek, a branch of the Chester river, to the head waters of Churn creek.[2]

"VESTRYMEN chosen for the s^d Parish & C^a vizt—
Mr William Frisby
Mr Michael Miller
Mr Hans Hanson
Mr Charles Tilden
Mr Thomas Smyth
Mr Simon Wilmore"

ST. PAUL'S CHURCH is the parish church and stands at the head of Dunn's creek, the Northwest branch of Langford's bay, amid a grove of giant oaks. The church was completed in 1713.

THE REV. STEPHEN BORDLEY was sent in 1697 to the parish to take up the work that had been begun by the Rev.Mr.Lawrence Vanderbush, the first minister. Mr. Vanderbush went to St. Paul's in September, 1693 and not only preached in this parish but also held services in South Sassafras or Shrewsbury parish. This latter parish was then within the bounds of Cecil county. The Rev. Stephen Bordley incumbent 1696.[3]

By an Act of the Assembly, passed April 4th, 1697, the division line between this and Shrewsbury parish was determined and a commission appointed to run the line and make a report to the Assembly. The bounds of St. Paul's parish were changed but little when the line was finally run in 1698; the commission finished its work that year. The following is a partial copy of the Act: "That from and after the tenth of June 1698 all that land and inhabitants in Chester river above the riding over of a branch of Morgan's Creek on the east side of William Bateman's house and on the north side of a line drawn from the riding over of the sd branch to the head of a branch of a Creek issueing out of the Bay called Churn Creek, be Always taken and reputed and be in Shrewsbury parish and All the land on the South side of the sd Churn Creek and Branch and Division line down the Bay to the extent of CECIL COUNTY be added to St. Paul's parish in KENT COUNTY on the North side of Chester River and Always to be Reputed in St. Paul's Parish any Law, Custom or Usage to the contrary Notwithstanding."
[1] Arch. Md., Vol. 23, p. 21.
[2] Arch. Md., Vol. 23, p. 21.
[3] B. C. Steiner in Md. Hist. Magazine, Vol. 12, p. 119.

ANNE ARUNDEL COUNTY

Named for Lady Anne Arundel, the wife of Cecilius Calvert, second Lord Baltimore.

ANNE ARUNDEL COUNTY'S (erected 1650) southern boundary was a "line from Herring Creek to the head of Patuxant River."[1]
No. 3

The Chesapeake bay was the eastern boundary and according to the Act of Assembly of 1722, Chap. No. 3, the division between Westminster parish in Anne Arundel and the parish of St. Paul's in Baltimore county apparently ran from the Chesapeake bay at a point about equidistant from the Magothy river and the mouth of Bodkin creek to about where the present village of Elkridge is situated. This line followed the ridge between the Patapsco and Magothy rivers. How long this line had served to divide the two parishes is not known.

The following official record shows that part of Anne Arundel belonged to Baltimore county in 1694:

"Petition of the Inhabitants Situated upon the South Side of the Patapsco River praying that they may be Rejoyned to the County of Ann Arrundell as formerly they were. Which being Read, Ordered that the said peticōn be sent to the house of Assembly for their considercōn."[2]

"By the Assembly, Oct., 3rd 1694.

The within Petition Read & Considered, Voted whether the South Side of Patapsco River be added to the County of Ann Arrundell or Remaine still as it is. Carried by Majority of votes to Remaine as it is."[3]

[1] Arch. Md., Vol. 19, p. 318.
[2] Arch. Md., Vol. 19, p. 31.
[3] Arch. Md., Vol. 19, p 69.

THE FIRST PARISHES OF THE PROVINCE OF MARYLAND 117

ST. PAUL'S PARISH "consists of the rest of the County."[1] The Chesapeake bay from Worton creek south to the Chester river bounded the parish on the west, the Chester river also bounded it on the south and east. The northern line ran from Morgan's creek, a branch of the Chester river, to the head waters of Churn creek.[2]

No. 4

"VESTRYMEN chosen for the s^d Parish & C^a vizt—
Mr William Frisby
Mr Michael Miller
Mr Hans Hanson
Mr Charles Tilden
Mr Thomas Smyth
Mr Simon Wilmore"

ST. PAUL'S CHURCH is the parish church and stands at the head of Dunn's creek, the Northwest branch of Langford's bay, amid a grove of giant oaks. The church was completed in 1713.

THE REV. STEPHEN BORDLEY was sent in 1697 to the parish to take up the work that had been begun by the Rev. Mr. Lawrence Vanderbush, the first minister. Mr. Vanderbush went to St. Paul's in September, 1693 and not only preached in this parish but also held services in South Sassafras or Shrewsbury parish. This latter parish was then within the bounds of Cecil county. The Rev. Stephen Bordley incumbent 1696.[3]

By an Act of the Assembly, passed April 4th, 1697, the division line between this and Shrewsbury parish was determined and a commission appointed to run the line and make a report to the Assembly. The bounds of St. Paul's parish were changed but little when the line was finally run in 1698; the commission finished its work that year. The following is a partial copy of the Act: "That from and after the tenth of June 1698 all that land and inhabitants in Chester river above the riding over of a branch of Morgan's Creek on the east side of William Bateman's house and on the north side of a line drawn from the riding over of the sd branch to the head of a branch of a Creek issueing out of the Bay called Churn Creek, be Always taken and reputed and be in Shrewsbury parish and All the land on the South side of the sd Churn Creek and Branch and Division line down the Bay to the extent of CECIL COUNTY be added to St. Paul's parish in KENT COUNTY on the North side of Chester River and Always to be Reputed in St. Paul's Parish any Law, Custom or Usage to the contrary Notwithstanding."

[1] Arch. Md., Vol. 23, p. 21.
[2] Arch. Md., Vol. 23, p. 21.
[3] B. C. Steiner in Md. Hist. Magazine, Vol. 12, p. 119.

ANNE ARUNDEL COUNTY

Named for Lady Anne Arundel, the wife of Cecilius Calvert, second Lord Baltimore.

ANNE ARUNDEL COUNTY'S (erected 1650) southern boundary was a "line from Herring Creek to the head of Patuxant River."[1]
No. 3
The Chesapeake bay was the eastern boundary and according to the Act of Assembly of 1722, Chap. No. 3, the division between Westminster parish in Anne Arundel and the parish of St. Paul's in Baltimore county apparently ran from the Chesapeake bay at a point about equidistant from the Magothy river and the mouth of Bodkin creek to about where the present village of Elkridge is situated. This line followed the ridge between the Patapsco and Magothy rivers. How long this line had served to divide the two parishes is not known.

The following official record shows that part of Anne Arundel belonged to Baltimore county in 1694:

"Petition of the Inhabitants Situated upon the South Side of the Patapsco River praying that they may be Rejoyned to the County of Ann Arrundell as formerly they were. Which being Read, Ordered that the said peticōn be sent to the house of Assembly for their considercōn."[2]

"By the Assembly, Oct., 3rd 1694.

The within Petition Read & Considered, Voted whether the South Side of Patapsco River be added to the County of Ann Arrundell or Remaine still as it is. Carried by Majority of votes to Remaine as it is."[3]

[1] Arch. Md., Vol. 19, p. 318.
[2] Arch. Md., Vol. 19, p. 31.
[3] Arch. Md., Vol. 19, p 69.

STATE HOUSE
ANNAPOLIS, ANNE ARUNDEL COUNTY
Here many of the laws affecting the early Church in the Province were enacted.

THE FIRST PARISHES OF THE PROVINCE OF MARYLAND 119

"ANN ARRUNDEL COUNTY is divided into Six Hundreds vizt
1. Town Neck Hundred
2. Middle Neck "
3. Broad " "
4. South River "
5. West " "
6. Herring Creek " "[1]

"ANN ARRUNDEL COUNTY is Divided into Four Parishes vizt—
Herring Creek Parish
South River "
Middle Neck "
Broad Neck " "[2]

IN THE REPORT to the Assembly on July 30th, 1694, Anne Arundel was said to contain:
"4 Parishes laid out
but noe churches built.
nor noe Minister."[3]

THE PARISHES in Anne Arundel county were divided by the rivers that emptied into the Chesapeake with the exception of Broad Neck, or Westminster, parish on its northern side. This parish was divided from St. Paul's parish in Baltimore county as described on page 138 of this book. Their western boundaries being the line run north from the branch of Mattawoman creek to the northern limits of the Province, as called for in naming the bounds of Piscataway parish in Charles county.[4]

THE COURT HOUSE for Anne Arundel county was built at Annapolis.

[1] Arch. Md., Vol. 23, p. 25.
[2] Arch. Md., Vol. 23, p. 19.
[3] Arch. Md., Vol. 20, p. 107.
[4] See description Piscataway Parish. Page 135

"HERRING CREEK PARISH consists of Herring Creek Hundred and the major part of West River Hundred."[1]

No. 5

"Beginning at ye Southmost bounds of South River Parish and bounding on ye East with ye bay of Chesapeake lieing down southerly to ye creeke called Fishing Creek then west with ye Said creeke to ye bounds of Ann Arundel and Calvert Countys to Lyons Creek then with the said creeke to Potuxent then up the said river to ye land called White Plaines to the Southernmost bounds of South River Parish"[2] and to the beginning.

"VESTRYMEN chosen for Herring Creek Parish, viz[t]—
Thomas Tench Esq[r]
M[r] Seth Biggs
Cap[t] William Holland
Cap[t] Robert Lockwood
M[r] James Rigbey
M[r] Nicholas Perret."[3]   (Turrett?)

HERRING CREEK (now known as St. James') CHURCH was built in 1765. The records of the parish go back to 1695.[4] When the vestry assumed charge of the parish they found an old church already standing. It was the church of the original Herring Creek Parish. "The vestry set about building a new edifice, the contract for which was given out in 1695."[5]

THE FIRST RECTOR of the parish was the Rev. Henry Hall. He served from 1695 until his death in 1721. He was regularly inducted May 7th 1698. Joseph Tilley was lay reader in 1696 and 1697.[6]

[1] Arch. Md., Vol. 23, p. 19.
[2] Church Life in Colonial Maryland, p. 63.
[3] Arch. Md., Vol. 23, p. 19.
[4] Old Brick Churches, Ridgely.
[5] Church Life in Colonial Maryland, Gambrall, p. 68 & 257
[6] Allen Ms., p. 18.

St. James, Built 1765
Herring Creek, Anne Arundel County

ALL HALLOWS, BUILT ABOUT 1727
SOUTH RIVER, ANNE ARUNDEL COUNTY

This church has been recently repaired. It succeeds one standing at the time of the Establishment.

"SOUTH RIVER PARISH consists of South River Hundred and a Small part of West River Hundred."[1]

No. 6

"VESTRYMEN Chosen for South River Parish:
Capt Hen. Hanslope
Mr John Gresham
Mr William Roper
Mr Edw. Burgess
Mr Walter Phelps
Mr John Watkins."[2]

"ALL HALLOWS CHURCH was built about 1727, succeeding an earlier one which antedated the Establishment. The Rev. Duell Pead performed the rites of baptism in this neighborhood from 1682 to 1690."[3] He preached by request a sermon, 1683, before the Provincial Assembly[4] at St. Mary's City.

THE REV. JOSEPH COLEBATCH served as first rector, beginning his work in 1695. He died in 1735.[5]

---

[1] Arch. Md., Vol. 23, p. 19.
[2] Arch. Md., Vol. 23, p. 19.
[3] Old Brick Churches. Ridgely
[4] See page 7 of this book.
[5] Allen Ms.

"MIDDLE NECK PARISH is Scituated betwixt South
River and Severn River."[1]

"VESTRYMEN for the s^d Parish chosen &^{ca} Viz^t
    Mr Thos. Bland
    Mr Richd Wharfield
    Mr Laurence Draper
    Mr Jacob Harness
    Mr Wm Brown
    Mr Corne. Howard."[2]

ST. ANN'S CHURCH was begun in 1696 and finished in 1699. Committee appointed by Governor Nicholson reported, October 2, 1696, that "We find by computation that the Building of the Church [St. Ann's] at Annapolis, according to the modell prescribed by his Excellency will not cost less than 1200 pounds Sterling."[3] Rebuilt in 1792 and again in 1858.

THE REV. PEREGRINE CONY was rector of this parish from 1696 to 1698. The Rev. James Wootton was rector from 1706 to Apr. 19, 1710.[4]

---

[1] Arch. Md., Vol. 23, p. 19.
[2] Arch. Md., Vol. 23, p. 20.
[3] Arch. Md., Vol. 19, p. 450.
[4] Allen Ms.

ST. ANN, BUILT 1699, REBUILT 1792 AND 1858.
MIDDLE NECK PARISH, ANNAPOLIS, ANNE ARUNDEL COUNTY

ST. MARGARET

WESTMINSTER PARISH, ANNE ARUNDEL COUNTY

The first church, built shortly after the Establishment, replaced with brick church, 1731. The present church erected near site of the second church.

"BROAD NECK PARISH is situated on the North Side
           of Severn River including Town Neck &
No. 8   Broad Neck Hundreds."[1] This is now known
           as Westminster Parish.

"VESTRYMEN for the s^d Parish Chosen, &^{ca} vizt
    Mr John Bennet
    Mr William Hopkins
    Mr Rob't Eagle
    Mr George Eager
    Mr Hugh Merrican
    Mr Edw. Fuller."[2]

THERE WAS A CHURCH prior to 1692 which stood on Severn Heights. It was destroyed by fire many years ago, the parish records perishing with the old church. A few tombstones and the stone foundation of the old church remain to mark the site.

THE REV. EDWARD TOPP, JR., was the first rector. The Rev. Edward Topp, Jr. was incumbent in 1696.[3] Dr. Ethan Allen[4] states that he (Topp) was there in 1698. He also states that the Rev. James Wootton was rector in 1705.

---

[1] Arch. Md., Vol. 23, p. 20.
[2] Arch. Md., Vol. 23, p. 20.
[3] B. C. Steiner in Md. Hist. Magazine, Vol. 12, p. 119.
[4] Allen Ms. p. 18.

CALVERT COUNTY

Named for the Calvert Family.

No. 4

CALVERT COUNTY (erected 1650) in 1692 was divided from Anne Arundel County "by a line from Herring Creek to the head of the Patuxent."[1] On the east the county was bounded by the Cheapeake bay. On the south and west by Pyne Hill creek, then paralleling the Three Notched Road and then on through the woods to the "head of the Patuxent." Calvert County in 1692 comprised parts of the present counties of St. Marys, Charles, Prince Georges and Anne Arundel.

"At that time the Governor decided to—'Erect make and appoint both sides of the Putuxent river into one County by the name of CALVERT COUNTY bounded on the Southside with Pynehill River or Creek to the head thereof and from thence through the woods to the head of Putexent River being the Northerly bound of St. Maries County and bounded on the North Side with the Creek upon the Westerne Side of Chesapeake Bay called the Herring Creeke and from thence through the woods to the head of Putuxent River being the Southerly bound of Anne Arundel County'."[2]

The two parishes of St. Paul's and All Faiths which were within the bounds of the old county were laid out on the west side of the Patuxent river.

"CALVERT COUNTY is divided into Six Hundreds, vizt—

Lyons Creeke	Hundred	Hunting Creek	Hundred
Lower End of Cliffs	"	Leonards Creek	"
Upper End of Cliffs	"	Elton Head	" "[3]

[1] Arch. Md., Vol. 23,
[2] The Counties of Maryland. Edward B. Mathews.
[3] Arch. Md., Vol. 23, p. 23.

MIDDLEHAM CHAPEL, BUILT 1748
CHRIST CHURCH PARISH, LUSBY, CALVERT COUNTY

ST. PAUL

PRINCE FREDERICK, CALVERT COUNTY

THE FIRST PARISHES OF THE PROVINCE OF MARYLAND

"CALVERT COUNTY is divided into Four Parishes, vizt
Christ Church
All Saints
St. Pauls
All Faiths."[1]

REPORT to the Assembly
July 30, 1694.

"CALVERT COUNTY has
5 parishes laid out,
3 whereof have Churches built,
but noe Ministers."[2]

THE FIRST COURT HOUSE for Calvert was the church at Mt. Calvert. "Ordered that it be moved to the Burgesses for a law that the church at Mount Calvert be a Court house as well as a Church."[3] Court House at Calvert Town 1694.[4]

---

[1] Arch. Md., Vol. 23, p. 18.
[2] Arch. Md., Vol. 20, p. 108.
[3] Arch. Md., Vol. 20, p. 284.
[4] Arch. Md., Vol. 20, p. 76.

"CHRIST CHURCH PARISH consists of these following Hundreds, vizt
No. 9 Hunting Creek Hundred
Leonards Creek do
Eltonhead do
Clifts Lower do "[1]

"VESTRYMEN chosen at the time and place [Waringtown], vizt:—
Mr Richd Smith
Capt Thomas Clegate
Mr Henry Firnley
Mr Francis Maulden
Mr John Manning
Mr Samuel Holdsworth"[2]

"THE CHURCH being already built [1692], called by the name of Christ Church standing on one acre of land gave by Mr. Francis Mauldin for the same Intent and purpose out his tract of land called by the name of 'Prevent Danger'."[3] Christ Church was rebuilt in 1735.

THE FIRST MINISTER was the Rev. Dr. William Mullett who preached in this vicinity in 1684.[4] The Rev. Mr. Turling was preaching there in 1691.[5] The Rev. Richard Hill was the minister of Christ Church Parish serving there in 1694.[6] The Rev. Henry Hall was rector 1695-1697.[7]

ONE SET OF THE LIBRARY books sent over to the Province by the Rev. Thomas Bray was sent to Mr. Richard Smith, a vestryman of Christ Church Parish.[8]

[1] Arch. Md., Vol. 23, p. 18.
[2] Arch. Md., Vol. 8, p. 472.
[3] Arch. Md., Vol. 8, p. 472.
[4] Arch. Md., Vol. 17,
[5] Allen Ms., p. 15.
[6] Allen Ms., p. 68.
[7] Allen Ms., p. 18.
[9] Arch. Md., Vol. 20, p. 212.

CHRIST, BUILT ABOUT 1735
PORT REPUBLIC, CALVERT COUNTY

ALL SAINTS

SUNDERLAND, CALVERT COUNTY

This church succeeds one built prior to 1695.

THE FIRST PARISHES OF THE PROVINCE OF MARYLAND 127

"ALL SAINTS PARISH consists of these two following Hundreds, vizt—
No. 10   Lyons Creek Hundred and the Upper hundred of the Clifts."[1]

"VESTRYMEN for the s^d Parish chosen &^{ca} vizt
Mr Walter Smith
Mr William Nichols
Mr William Turner
Mr John Scott
Mr John Leech Junr
Mr John Hance."[2]

"AND A CHURCH to be built on one acre of land belonging to Thomas Kemp on the cross Road of Severn Ridge Path and the road leading to Cox town to be called by the name of All Saints Church."[3]
    "Petition of the vestrymen of the parish of All Saints in Calvert County sitting forth that they had taken care to build a church within their said parish and had sometimes on Sunday in an afternoon the benefit of Mr Hull's preaching amongst them, etc."[4]   The present church was built in 1815.

REV. HENRY HALL officiated in 1694.[5]   "Mr Andrew Geddes, layreader at All Saints October 8th 1696."[6] Mr. Thomas Cockshutt was appointed minister in 1697.

"AN ACC^T OF THE SIX SETS OF BOOKS the Bishop of London sent and where they are and to whom delivered to.   To Walter Smith, vestryman of the church newly built in the freshes of the Patuxent where Mr Hull intends to preach.."[7]

[1] Arch. Md., Vol. 23, p. 18.
[2] Arch. Md., Vol. 23, p. 18.
[3] Arch. Md., Vol. 8, p. 473.
[4] Arch. Md., Vol. 20, p. 277.
[5] Allen Ms. p. 18.
[6] Arch. Md., Vol. 20, p. 515.
[7] Arch. Md., Vol. 20, p. 212.

"ST. PAUL'S PARISH consists of the following bounds, vizt

No. 11 From the Upper Part of Mt Calvert hundred to the main branch of Swantsons Creek."[1] This was decided at a "Court held at Benedict Leonard Town the 14th of February, 1693."

"VESTRYMEN for the s^d Parish chosen &^{ca} vizt
Mr Thomas Brooke
Mr Thomas Greenfield
Mr Thomas Hollyday
Mr Richd Charlet
Mr William Barton
Mr Saml Magruther."[2]   [Magruder]

"THE CHURCH for the same [parish] being already built [1692] at Charles Town called by the name of St. Paul's Church."[3]

REV. MR. TURLING was rector prior to 1691.[4] The encumbent in 1696 was Monsieur Morien.[5] Rev. Thos. Davis was rector in 1695,[6] and the Rev. Robert Owen, from 1700 to 1710.

QUEEN ANNE PARISH in 1704 was erected from this parish by Act of the Assembly, Chapter 96.[7]

"ONE SET OF BOOKS to Thomas Hollyday vestryman of the church at Mount Calvert for that church."[8]

---

[1] Arch. Md., Vol. 23, p. 18.
[2] Arch. Md., Vol. 23, p. 18.
[3] Arch. Md., Vol. 8, p. 473.
[4] Allen Ms. p. 15
[5] B. C. Steiner, Md. Hist. Mag., Vol. 12, p. 118.
[6] Allen Ms., p. 18.
[7] Bacon's Laws of Maryland.
[8] Arch. Md., Vol. 20, p. 212.

ST. PAUL, BUILT 1733
BADEN, PRINCE GEORGE'S COUNTY
Sun dial placed on this church in 1753. It is the only church that was so adorned.

ALL FAITH, BUILT 1765

MECHANICSVILLE, ST. MARY'S COUNTY

This one succeeds a church which was standing at the time of the Establishment.

"ALL FAITHS PARISH consists of the following bounds, vizt
No. 12   From the main branch of Swanson's Creek to the Lower part of Harvy Hundred."[1]

"VESTRYMEN for the s^d Parish chosen, &^{ca} vizt
Mr James Keech
Mr John Smith
Mr Rich'd Southern [Sotheron]
Mr John Gillam
Mr Charles Askue [Ashcom?]
Capt Richd Gardner."[2]

"THE CHURCH for the said Parish being already built standing by the fork of Trent Creek called by the name of All Faiths Church."[3] The present church erected 1765.

"REV. MR. TURLING minister prior to 1691."[4] The Rev. Thomas Davis went there as rector in 1695.[5]

TRINITY PARISH was erected out of part of this parish by Act of the Assembly, 1744, Chapter 14.[6]

---

[1] Arch. Md., Vol. 23, p. 18.
[2] Arch. Md., Vol. 23, p. 18.
[3] Arch. Md., Vol. 8, p. 474.
[4] Allen Ms. p. 15.
[5] Allen Ms., p. 18.
[6] Bacon's Laws of Maryland.

CHARLES COUNTY

Named for Charles Calvert, Third Lord Baltimore

CHARLES COUNTY (erected 1658) in 1692 was bounded on the south and west by St. Mary's county No. 5 and the Potomac river, on the east by Calvert county and the north by the Maryland-Pennsylvania line. This may be more fully described by quoting from Thomas' Chronicles of Colonial Maryland: "Charles County bounds, the river Wicomico to its head and from the mouth of that River up the Potomac as high as the settlements extend and thence to the head of Wicomico." In describing the bounds of Piscataway Parish, the northernmost of the Charles county parishes, Dr. Allen gives practically all of the rest of the Province (not already covered by the other nine counties) to this county thereby making it nearly equal in area to all the other counties combined.

"CHARLES COUNTY is divided into Seven hundreds, vizt

Lower part of William & Mary Parish   Hundred.
Upper   "   "   "   "   "   "   "
East Side of Portobacco   "
West   "   "   "   "
Lower part of Nanjemy Parish   "
Upper   "   "   "   "
Upper   "   " King & Queen Parish[1]   "
   Benedict Town being joyned to part of King & Queen Parish."[2]

---

[1] This Hundred counted as part of St. Mary's until 1716. Was also known as Newport Hundred.
[2] Arch. Md., Vol. 23, p. 24.

ST. PAUL, BUILT 1775
ROCK CREEK PARISH, DISTRICT OF COLUMBIA

This church was destroyed by fire in 1921. It was built at the time the Rev. Alexander Williamson was rector and succeeded one built prior to 1726 at which time Prince George's Parish was laid out, Prince George's Parish being the first division of Piscattoway or St. John's Parish. Piscattoway Parish embraced all of Western Maryland including the territory now within the District of Columbia. The National Capitol and the National Cathedral are standing now in what was Piscattoway Parish.

THE FIRST PARISHES OF THE PROVINCE OF MARYLAND 131

"CHARLES COUNTY is divided into four Parishes vizt
>William & Mary
>Port Tobacco
>Nanjemy
>Piscatoway, the Bounds whereof being artificial and Somewhat Long have Omitted to insert them here."[1]

REPORT to the Assembly;
>July 30, 1694.
>"Charles County has 4 parishes laid out, vizt
>>William and Mary, which has church built
>>Portobacco, which has church built
>>Nanjemie, which has church building
>>Pescattaway, which has a church agreed for
>>All want ministers, Vestry men in every Parish."[2]

THE COURT HOUSE for Charles County stood (1688) on the plantation of Thomas Hussey. "Ordered that the Deputy Surveyor of Charles County survey and lay out the Lott or Acre of Land on which the Court House in the said County standeth including in the said Acre said Court House, Prison, Pillory and Stocks . . . . in no wise prejudiceing the dwelling or the other houses of the said Thomas Hussey near the said Court House adjacent . . " April 5, 1688.[3]

---

[1] Arch. Md., Vol. 23, p. 18.
[2] Arch. Md., Vol. 20, p. 109, and Md. Cal. of Wills, Vol. 1, p. 48.
[3] Arch. Md., Vol. 8, p. 26.

WILLIAM AND MARY PARISH bounds are given in the court records of Charles County. Dr. Allen's No. 13 Ms described them as follows: "Bounds of Pickawaxon Parish. Beginning at the plantation of John Courtes, Senior, and running with a straight line to the plantation formerly Samuel Cresseyes' Landing— the said COURTES on the north of the said line and the said CRESSEYES on the southside of the said line and bounding with the Potomac River to the mouth of Wiccomomico River and so up the Wiccomomico to the head of said river and with the branch thereof to the said Courtes' Point."[1]

"VESTRYMEN for William & Mary Parish chosen,&c^a vizt
Col^l John Courts
Mr Robert Yates
Mr William Hawton
Mr Henry Hardy
Mr John Wielder
Mr William Harbert."[2]

CHRIST CHURCH. The first church was built prior to 1691.[3]

DR. ETHAN ALLEN states that the Rev. Mr. Moore was rector of the parish in 1692 and 1693 and the Rev. George Tubman preached from 1695 to 1700.[4]

---

[1] Charles County Land Records, Lib. R., p. 459.
[2] Arch. Md., Vol. 23, p. 19.
[3] Allen Ms., p. 15.
[4] Allen Ms., p. 18.

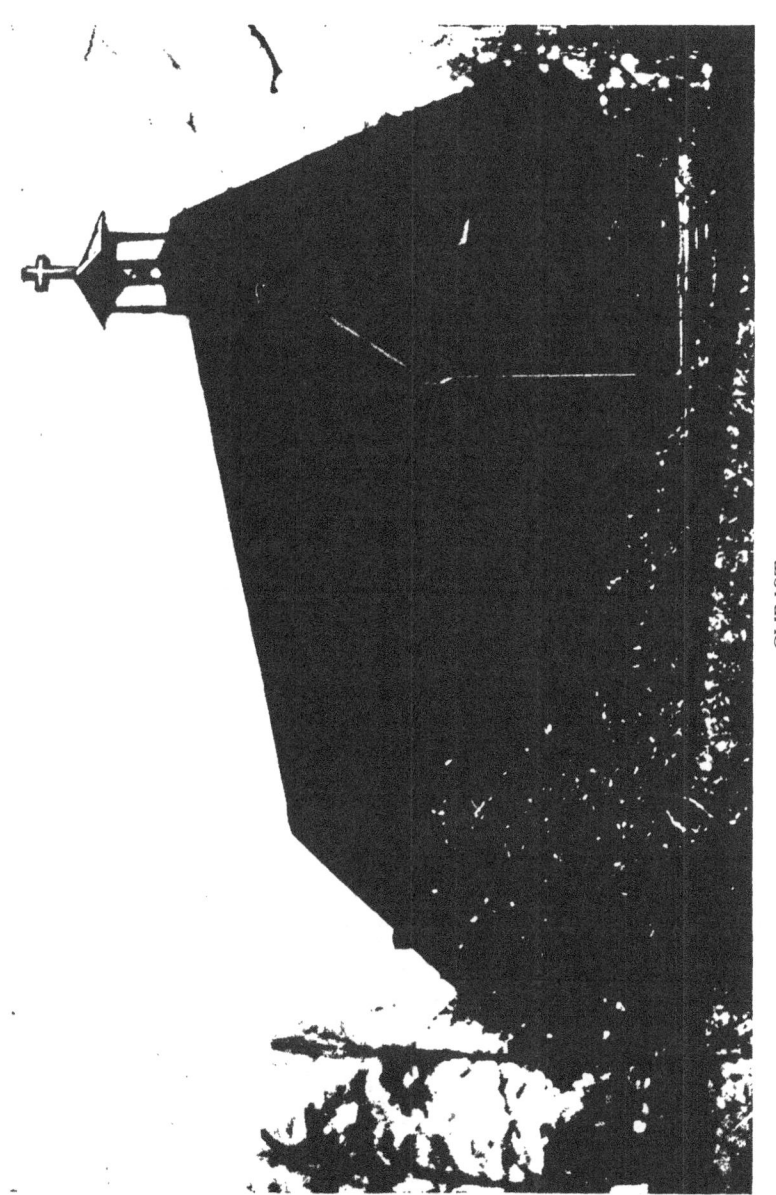

CHRIST
WAYSIDE, CHARLES COUNTY
Parish Church of William and Mary Parish, also called Piccawaxon Parish

CHRIST

LA PLATA, CHARLES COUNTY

Representing old Port Tobacco Parish Church, which was built of brick in 1753 at Portobacco. It succeeded one standing about the time of the Establishment.

THE FIRST PARISHES OF THE PROVINCE OF MARYLAND 133

PORT TOBACCO PARISH is described in Dr. Allen's Ms as follows: "Beginning at the plantation of No. 14 Samuel Cresseyes and running up the Potomac River to the mouth of Nanjemy Creek or Avon River and so up the Nanjemy Creek to the Mill at the head thereof and so up the said branch to Capt. Hoskin's Quarter and then with a straight line to the head of Joseph Bullett's Mill Branch and down the said Branch to Mattawoman Creek, thence up the Mattawoman Creek to the utmost limits of the County [Charles] to the head of Zachyah Branch and with the said Branch to John Courtes, Senior, and with the line of Pickyawaxan Parish [William and Mary] to Cresseyes plantation."[1]

"VESTRYMEN for Port Tobacco Parish chosen &^{ca}vizt
Mr Henry Hawkins
Mr William Barton
Mr Phil Hoskins
Mr C. Lomax
Mr John Hawkins
Mr John Hanson."[2]

"AND IN CHARLES COUNTY att the head of Portobacco Creeke [April 26, 1684] neare the Church there."[3] Notice that this church was built prior to the Establishment, and according to Dr. Allen was called "Christ Church."

THE REV. MR. MOORE preached there in 1691, 1692 and 1693.[4] The Rev. George Tubman was rector in 1695, he also was rector of William and Mary & Nanjemy Parishes at the same time. He died in 1701.[5]

[1] Charles County Land Records, Lib. R, p. 460.
[2] Arch. Md., Vol. 23, p. 19.
[3] Arch. Md., Vol. 13, p. 112.
[4] Allen Ms., p. 18.
[5] Allen Ms., p. 65.

NANJEMY PARISH which is now known as "Durham Parish" is bounded as follows:—"Beginning at Phillip Hoskin's Quarter, soe with a straight line to the head of Joseph Bullett's Mill Branch and down the said Branch to Mattawoman Creeke and so down Mattawoman Creek to the mouth thereof, and down the Potomak River to the mouth of Nanjemy Creek or Avon River and so up the said creek or river to the Mill at the head thereof and thence to Capt. Hoskin's Quarter."[1]

No. 15

"VESTRYMEN for Nanjemy Parish chosen &^{ca} vizt
    Mr John Stone
    Mr Joseph Manning
    Mr William Dent
    Mr William Stone
    Mr Richard Harrison
    Mr Gerrard Fowke."[2]

THE CHURCH for this Parish was being built at the time the report was made to the Assembly.[3] Upon completion it was called Durham Church. The second church (now standing) was authorized to be built in 1732.

REV. JOHN TURLING, "Presbyter Anglicans", probably first Rector of this parish. William Dent and Elizabeth Fowke were married by him in 1684.[4] Rev. George Tubman rector in 1695.[5] Rev. George Tubman incumbent in 1696.[6]

[1] Allen Ms.
[2] Arch. Md., Vol. 23, p. 19.
[3] Arch. Md., Vol. 20, p. 109.
[4] Charles County Court Records, Liber R No. 1, Vol. 2.
[5] Allen Ms., p. 18.
[6] B. C. Steiner in Md. Hist. Magazine, Vol. 12, p. 118.

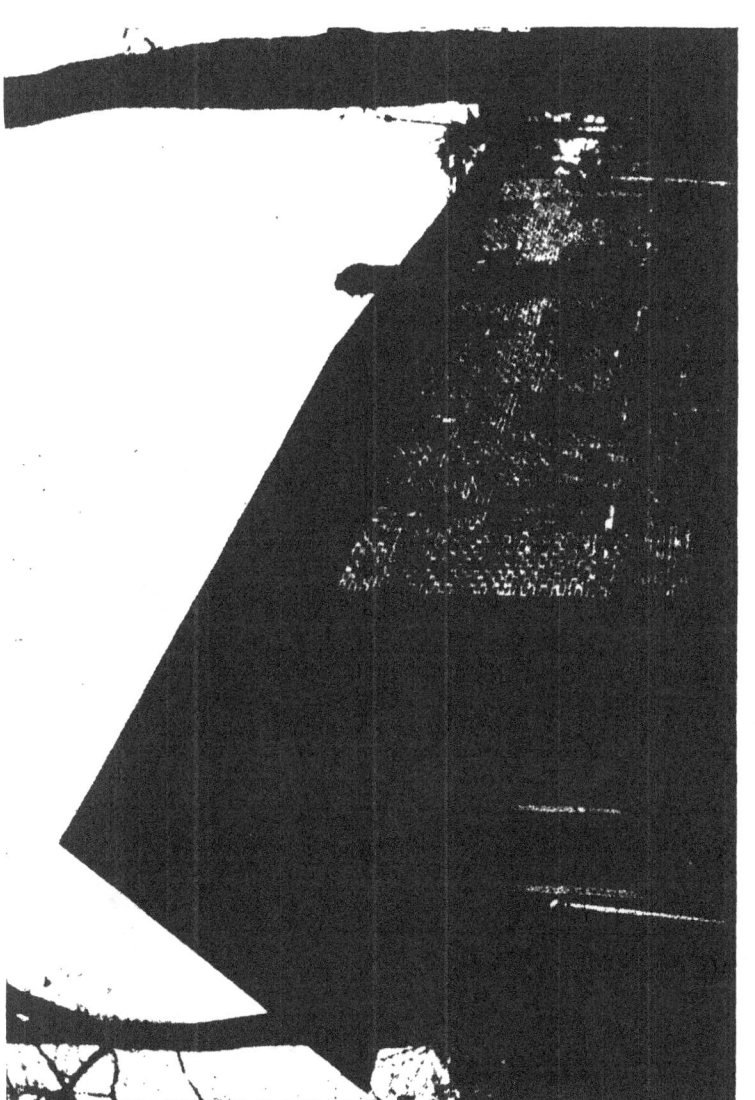

CHRIST, BUILT ABOUT 1732
GRAYTON, CHARLES COUNTY
Parish Church of Nanjemoy or Durham Parish.

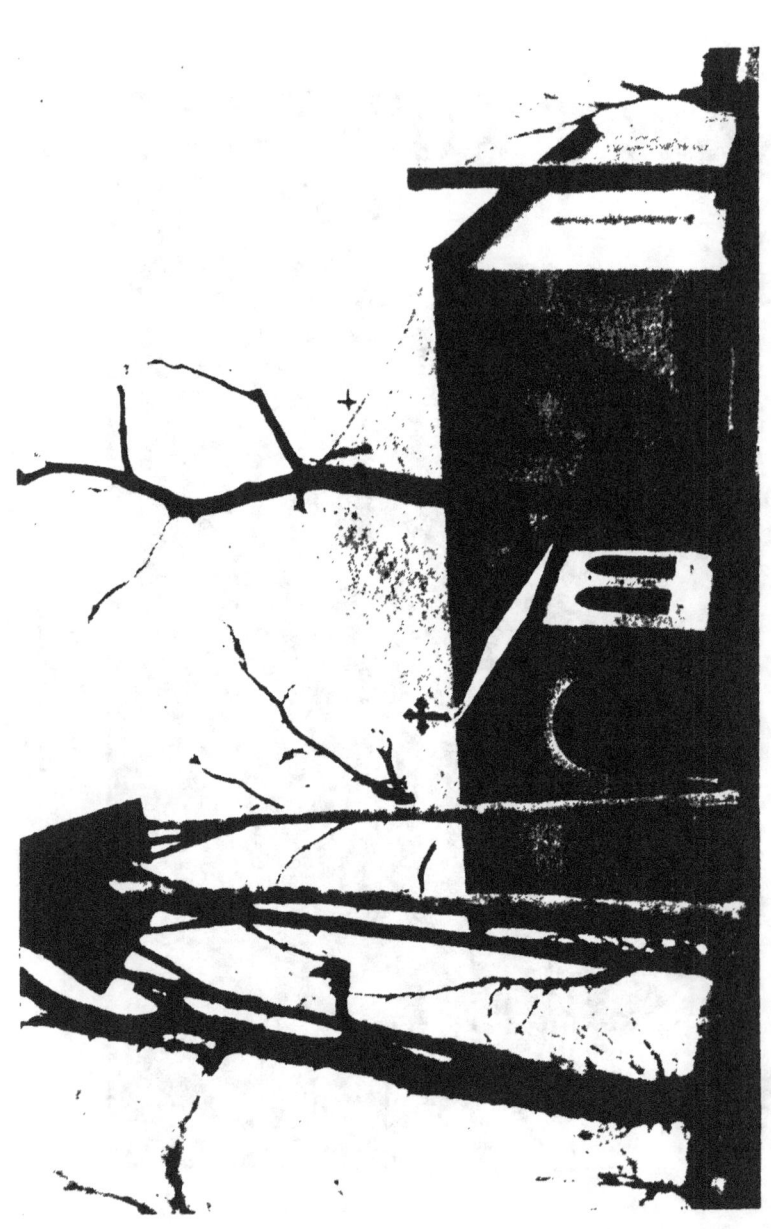

ST. JOHN, BUILT ABOUT 1723
BROAD CREEK, PRINCE GEORGE'S COUNTY
Parish Church of Piscattoway Parish. This church succeeded the first parish church, built 1699.

PISCATTAWAY PARISH (alias St. John's.) Doctor Allen gives the bounds of this parish as follows: "Beginning at the mouth of the Mattawoman Creek and running up the said Creek and Branch thereof to the utmost limits of the County [Charles] and running North to the line of the Province and then West to the Potomac River and then down the said River to the mouth of the Mattawoman Creek."[1]

No. 16

"VESTRYMEN for Piscattaway Parish chosen &^{ca} vizt[2]
John Addison Esqr
Mr William Hutchinson
Mr William Hatton
Mr William Tanneyhill
Mr John Emmet
Mr James Stoddart"[3]

NO CHURCH had been built at the time the report was made. The first meeting of the vestry was held at the house of John Addison, Esqr. At that meeting it was decided to buy 78 acres, part of "Lisle Hall", at Broad Creek. It was on this land in 1699 that the parish church was built and it received the name of "Broad Creek Church."

PRINCE GEORGE'S PARISH[4], by Act of the Provincial Assembly, 1726, Chapter 6, was erected out of Piscattaway Parish, and the chapel of Ease at Rock

---

[1] Charles County Land Records, Liber R, p. 460.
[2] Arch. Md., Vol. 23, p. 19.
[3] Mr. John Smallwood was elected a member of the vestry on January 30th, 1693 and upon his death Mr. James Stoddart was elected July 29th, 1696 to fill the vacancy.
[4] Bacon's Laws of Maryland

Creek, built in 1719, became the parish church of Prince George's parish. In 1742 the Assembly was again petitioned further to divide the territory originally covered by Piscattaway Parish, and Chapter 18 of that Session erected "All Saints Parish" with the parish church at Frederick.[1]

THE FIRST RECTOR of Piscattaway Parish was the Rev. George Tubman who began his work August 4th, 1696. He was also rector of Portobacco, William and Mary and Nanjemy Parishes at the same time. He died in 1701.[2]

---

[1] Bacon's Laws.
[2] Dr. Ethan Allen's Ms., p. 65.

ALL SAINTS
FREDERICK CITY, FREDERICK COUNTY

The creation of All Saints Parish in 1742 was at tne expense of Prince George's Parish. The latter was itself taken from the original territory of Old Piscattoway Parish, which thus suffered its first dismemberment. The first All Saints Church was built in 1750; the new church was begun in 1855.

RECTORY, BUILT 1791
ST. PAUL'S PARISH, BALTIMORE

BALTIMORE COUNTY

Named for the Lord Baltimore's Irish Barony.

No. 6

BALTIMORE COUNTY (erected 1659) in 1692 was bounded on the east by the Susquehanna river. The Chesapeake bay was one of its boundaries. For its southern boundary, we quote proclamation of June 6th, 1674, "the southern boundary of Baltimore county shall be the south side of Potapsco River, and from the highest plantation on that side of the river due south two miles into the woods."[1]

This "two miles into the woods" means that a two mile strip of country on the south side of the Patapsco river was taken from Anne Arundel county by this "proclamation" for we find in the "Upper House Journal" under date of April 23, 1684 "A Petition of the Inhabitants scituate upon the southside of Patapsco River and others holding land there desireing to bee restored into the County of Ann Arundell from whence at first they were taken into Baltimore County by reason of their greate distance from and incommodious wayes of goeing to the County Court of Baltimore & Ca. Read and rejected,—This House Considering that Baltimore County being already very small and for other motives the same remaine as now it is."[2]

The present southern boundary of Baltimore county was made by Act of Assembly 1722, Chap. 3, and the former lines recited in the Act prove that the division line between the two counties, Baltimore and Anne Arundel, began upon the shore of the Chesapeake bay about a mile and a quarter south of Bodkin Point and paralleled the

[1] Scharf's Hist. of Baltimore County, p. 41.
[2] Arch. Md., Vol. 13, p. 41.

course of the Patapsco at a distance of about two miles, running northwest along the ridge between the Magothy and the Patapsco rivers.

The western boundary[1] of the county was the line that bounded Piscattaway parish (Charles county) on the east—this line ran north from the head of Mattawoman creek to the boundary line of the Province.

THE FIRST COURT HOUSE of Baltimore county was built on Bush river, now Harford county, and it is generally supposed it was there that the Court met until 1712 when by Act of Assembly the Court House was built in Joppa, also now in Harford county. In 1768 the Court House was abandoned and the county seat removed to Baltimore city.[2]

"BALTIMORE COUNTY is divided into Five Hundreds, vizt

Speceutia	Hundred
Gun Powder River	"
South Side Gun Powder	"
North Side Patapsco	"
South Side Patapsco	" " [3]

REPORT to the Assembly, June 30, 1694. "What Parishes laid out unknown." "The division of the Parishes and Bounds thereof have not as yet been Returned by the Clerk of the said County but do find by the Returns of the Severall Vestrymen that the said County is divided into three Parishes, vizt

Patapsco [St. Paul's] Parish	
St John's	"
St Georges	" " [4]

---

[1] Note Baltimore County's western boundary.
[2] Scharf's Hist. of Baltimore County, p. 43.
[3] Arch. Md., Vol. 23, p. 24.
[4] Arch. Md., Vol. 23, p. 20.

VESTRY HOUSE, BUILT 1766

St. George's Parish, Perryman, Harford County

One of two such buildings erected in that year; the other one is at St. Paul's Church, Kent County.

ST. THOMAS, BUILT 1743

GARRISON FOREST, BALTIMORE COUNTY

Parish Church of St. Thomas' Parish laid out in 1742; the first division of St. Paul's Parish, Baltimore. This church succeeded a chapel of ease built prior to 1740.

THE FIRST PARISHES OF THE PROVINCE OF MARYLAND 139

In accordance with the directions of this Act of the Assembly, (1692, Ch. 2) the Justices of Baltimore County at a Court held Nov. 1692 made the following order:—"That one Parish be in Speceutia Hundred, and another in Gunpowder River (that is to say) from Gunpowder River to the head of Middle River And [another] from Middle River as far as the County goes or extends."[1]

June 27, 1702.

"According to his Excellency the Governour's order and summons appeared the Vestry of St. Paul's Parish on Patapsco River in Baltimore County and it being required of them to produce their Accounts how the 40 lb. p poll raised in that Parish has been disposed of Mr Richard Cromwell alledges for that the Sheriff of the County Lieut. Col^l Maxwell is now very sick but says that the Vestry have about 20000 pounds of Tob° wherewith they desire to build a Chappel of Ease for the Parishioners on the South side of Patapsco River but that being contrary to Law.

Ordered by his Excell^{cy} the Governour & Council that the said Vestry do apply what Tob° they have in their Hands belonging to the Parish in building a pretty convenient House and purchasing a Glebe for the Minister & his successors."[2]

---

[1] Baltimore County Court Records, Vol. F, p. 338.
[2] Arch. Md., Vol. 24, p. 289.

No. 17

"PATAPSCO (or St. Paul's) PARISH. The bounds of this parish were as follows:—On the east by Middle river, on the south by the Chesapeake bay, on the west by the county of Anne Arundel and the eastern boundry line of Piscattaway parish,[1] one of the parishes of Charles County. It was bounded on the north by the boundry line of the province.

"THE VESTRY, September 1693, was as follows:—
    George Ashman   Richard Sampson
    John Ferry   Richard Cromwell
    Nicholas Corban   Francis Watkings
        John Gay, Clerk to the Vestry"[2]

THE FIRST CHURCH built, 1702, in this parish stood at the head of "Cloppers," now Colgate creek. "We the Vestrie men for Patapsco Hundred met together at the house of Major John Thomas [resolved] that at Pettites Old Field was the most convenient place for to erect a Church."[3]

    The present parish church stands on the corner of Charles and Saratoga Streets in the City of Baltimore. The first church built on this site was erected in 1730.

THE REV. EDWARD TOPP, JR. was the incumbent of this parish in 1696.[4] According to the Allen Manuscript the first rector of the parish was the Rev. Edward Topp, Jr. He served from 1698 to 1702.

ST. THOMAS' PARISH was the first subdivision of St. Paul's Parish. It was erected by authority of an Act of the Provincial Assembly in 1742, Chapter 15.[5]

---
[1] See bounds of Piscattaway Parish, Charles County.
[2] Court Records, Baltimore County, Liber G, No. 1, p. 126.
[3] Court Records, Baltimore County, Liber G, No. 1, p. 126.
[4] B. C. Steiner in Maryland Hist. Mag., Vol. 12, p. 119.
[5] Bacon's Laws of Maryland.

ST. PAUL, BUILT 1856

St. Paul's Parish, Baltimore City

This is the fifth parish church to have been built in St. Paul's Parish and the fourth on this spot. The first church stood on "Cloppers," now Colgate Creek.

ST. JOHN, BUILT 1815

KINGSVILLE, BALTIMORE COUNTY

Old Parish Church of Copley or St. John's Parish. The first church of this parish was built at Joppa, once county seat of Baltimore County.

ST. JOHN'S PARISH ("alias Copley Parish"), Dr. Allen says, contained the two hundreds of Gunpowder and Southern Gunpowder, bounded, according to the best records obtainable, by the Bush river on the east, the Chesapeake bay on the South, Middle river on the west and the northern line of the Province on the north.

No. 18

Dr. Allen's Ms. gives the following as vestrymen in June 1693.
Mr Thomas Haley
Mr Thomas Hodge
Mr Richard Adams
Mr Moses Groome
Capt Thomas Preston
Mr Lawrence Richardson.

"VESTRYMEN chosen as by Return, vizt
Mr Thomas Staley
Capt Thomas Preston
Mr Richard Adams
Mr Samuel Siclemore
Mr Daniel Scott
Mr Abram Tayler."[1]

"THE CHURCH to be on Elk Neck on Gunpowder River."[2] St. Johns Church was built later at the former county seat of Baltimore county, Joppa, but the present parish church is at Kingsville, built in 1817.

IT IS KNOWN THAT the famous Rev. John Yeo, who died in 1686, lived in the territory which was included in 1692 in the parish bounds. The earliest record of a minister after the Establishment is that of the Rev. John Edwards, 1710.

ST. JAMES PARISH was erected in 1770, the chapel of ease of St. John's Parish becoming the parish church.

[1] Arch. Md., Vol. 23, p. 20.
[2] Dr. Allen's Ms.

ST. GEORGE'S PARISH was bounded on the east and south by the Susquehanna river and Chesapeake bay. The Bush river and its headwaters served as the western bounds. The northern line of the Province was its northern limits.

No. 19

"VESTRYMEN as by Return, vizt
  Mr William Hollace [Wallace?]
  Mr Laurence Tayler
  Mr John Parker
  Mr George Smith
  Mr Roger Mathews
  Mr Thomas Cordey."[1]

THE FIRST CHURCH in this part of the Province was called "Spesutia Church" built in 1671.[2] This present church is now called St. George's and is near the village of Perryman, Harford county.

THE REV. JEREMIAH EATON was the first Protestant minister in Baltimore county (west of the Chesapeake bay) and he owned land (1675) near Bush river. In 1683 the Rev. John Yeo preached in that part of Baltimore county afterwards laid out into St. George's Parish. He settled at New Castle, Delaware, June 4, 1678, and was the first Episcopal minister in that State. Rev. Thomas Dawes "min- of this parish, 1695;[3] Rev. Jno. Edwards rector 1702–1711;[4] Rev. Evan Evans from 1718 to 1722.[5]

---

[1] Arch. Md., Vol. 23, p. 20.
[2] Allen Ms., p. 18.
[3] Arch. Md., Vol. 19, p. 274.
[4] Allen Ms., pp. 19–20.
[5] Allen Ms., p. 71.

ST. GEORGE, BUILT 1851
PERRYMAN, HARFORD COUNTY

It is the third church on this spot and the fourth one of the Parish. The first parish church was built on "Walstons Addition" near Delf Creek in what is now Harford County.

CHRIST
Easton, Talbot County
The Parish Church of St. Peter's Parish, of which the corner stone was laid May 21, 1840.

TALBOT COUNTY

Named for Grace Talbot, daughter of George Calvert, first Lord Baltimore.

No. 7

TALBOT COUNTY (erected 1662) in 1692 extended from the head of Chester river down to the Choptank river. The western bounds were the Chester river, the "Narrows," Eastern bay and the Chesapeake.

While the eastern boundaries were identical with those of the Province there were very few colonists who lived far from the water courses, hence the eastern limits were not sharply defined.

"TALBOT COUNTY is divided into nine Hundreds, vizt
  Tredhaven   Hundred
  Bullinbroake   "
  Mill   "
  Tuckohoe   "
  Worrell   "
  Bay   "
  Island   "
  Chester   "
  Lower of Kent Island. "   " [1]

"TALBOT COUNTY is divided into three Parishes, vizt
  St Paul's Parish
  St Peter's   "
  St Michael's   "   " [2]

---

[1] Arch. Md., Vol. 23, p. 24.
[2] Arch. Md., Vol. 23, p. 21.

REPORT to the Assembly
June 30, 1694. "They can Give noe certain Returne as yet for Talbot County."[1]

At a court held at Yorke, June 20th, 1693, there were appointed by the court the vestrymen for the three parishes of the County.[2]

THE FIRST COURT HOUSE was on Skipton creek, a branch of the Wye river, at "Hopton."[3]

" . . at the time of laying out the parishes, in 1693, the Court House was on a branch of Wye river where is the dwelling plantation of Mr. Wm. Hemsley Junr which by many is still called the old Court House."[4]

"In 1680 a Court House was built upon land purchased of Jonathan Hopkin which was located on Skipton creek near the headwaters of the Wye river. In this building court was held for the first time in 1682 or 1683. Later a 'prison' was built. Around these two buildings there grew up quite a village which was called, by Act of Assembly of 1686, "Yorke" evidently in honor of the ancient town in England of the same name."[5]

---

[1] Arch. Md., Vol. 20, p. 111.
[2] Ms. of Dr. Samuel A. Harrison.
[3] Hist. of Talbot County. Col. Oswald Tilghman,
[4] Ms. Dr. Samuel A. Harrison.
[5] Maryland's Colonial Eastern Shore, p. 26.

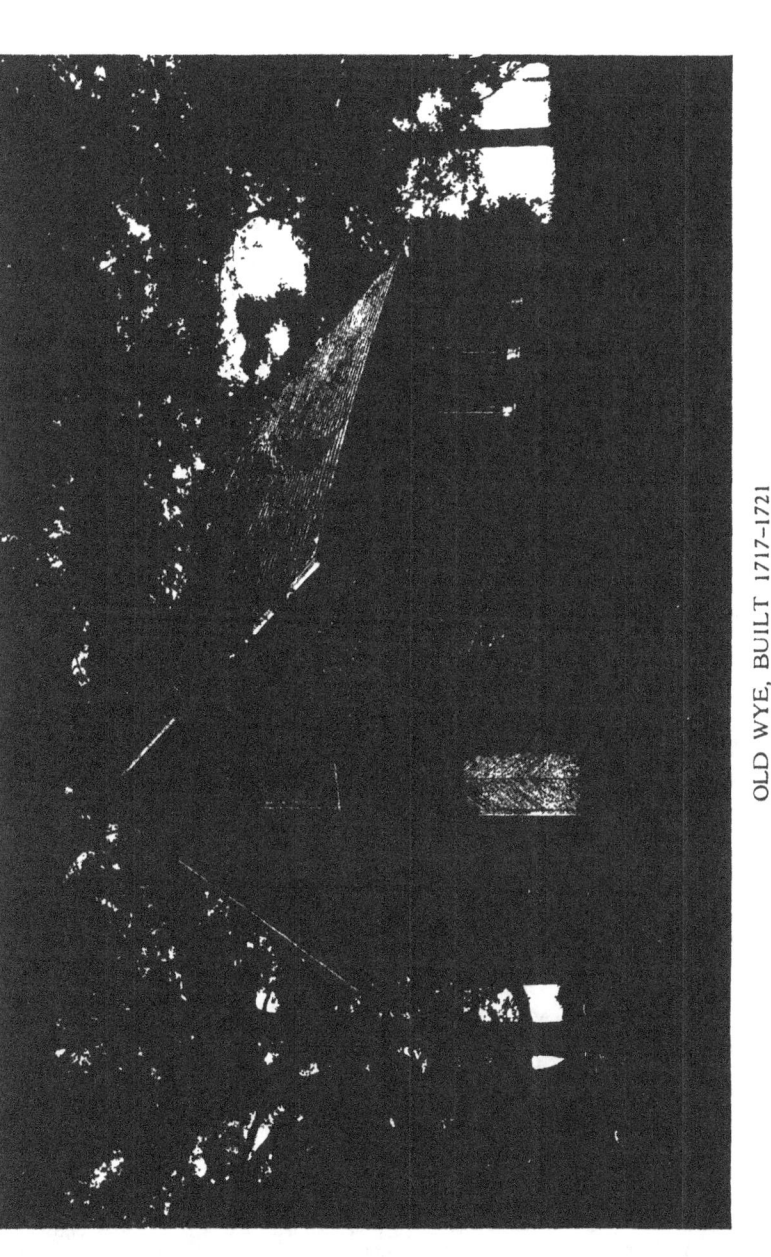

OLD WYE, BUILT 1717-1721
WYE MILLS, TALBOT COUNTY

This was a Chapel of Ease of St. Paul's Parish, Talbot County (after 1706 Queen Anne's County) until 1860 at which time it became the parish church of Wye Parish.

ST. PAUL, BUILT 1834
CENTERVILLE, QUEEN ANNE'S COUNTY

The first church of St. Paul's Parish was of wood construction and stood about a mile southwest of where Centerville is, at a place called "Hibernia." In 1698 this building was replaced by a brick structure and called "Chester" church. In 1765 Chester Church was in such bad condition that the vestry decided to rebuild it following the plans of St. Paul's Church in Philadelphia. This later building was torn down and some of the bricks, for sentimental reasons, were used in making the walls of the present parish church.

THE FIRST PARISHES OF THE PROVINCE OF MARYLAND 145

No. 20
"S^T PAUL'S PARISH begins at the head of Chester River & Extends to the Court House[1] and from the Court House along the north side of Brewers' Branch [now Skipton creek] to the Head of s^d branch and from thence to Judwin's branch being the North part of Tuccohoe Hundred."[2]

"VESTRYMEN for the S^d Parish chosen & C^a vizt
  Mr William Finney
  Mr William Coursey
  Mr John Whittington
  Mr Nathanial Wright
  Mr Robert Macklin
  Mr John Chairs."[3]

THE CHURCH for this parish was old Chester Church built near the present town of Centerville. It was torn down in 1834 and rebuilt in that town. In 1717 the vestry began the Chapel of Ease, now Wye Church, which is in excellent repair and stands almost hidden from view amongst some of the largest oaks to be seen anywhere on the Eastern Shore. This became the parish church, in 1860, of Wye Parish formed at that time.

THE REV. JOHN LILLINGSTON was minister from 1691 to 1709 when he died. He had held services in Talbot county as early as 1681.[4]

"ONE SET OF BOOKS to Mr. Lillingston sent by the Bishop of London 1694."[5]

ST. LUKE'S PARISH was taken from this parish by Act of Assembly 1728, Chapter 19.[6]

[1] On "Hopton" surveyed for Jonathan Hopkins, June, 1668.
[2] Arch. Md., Vol. 23, p. 21.
[3] Arch. Md., Vol. 23, p. 21.
[4] Ms. of Dr. Samuel A. Harrison.
[5] Arch. Md. Vol. 20, p. 212.
[6] Bacon's Laws of Maryland.

"ST. PETER'S PARISH begins at John Judwins Branch and extends to Oxford Town."[1]

No. 21 "In 1714 the county surveyor of Talbot County was authorized to 'lay off' the line of this parish and in his report to the Justices of the County says, 'St. Peter's Parish to contain Third Haven-Hundred, Bolingbroke Hundred and part of Tuckahoe Hundred bounding on the north by a line drawn from the head of Brewers' Branch, [now Skipton Creek], north 75 degrees east to the head of Judwin's Branch."[2]

"VESTRYMEN for the s^d Parish Chosen, &^{ca} vizt
  Mr Thomas Robins
  Mr Thomas Bowdle
  Mr George Robins
  Mr Nicholas Lowe
  Mr Samuel Abbet S^r
  Mr Thomas Martin."[3]

WHITEMARSH CHURCH, the ruins of which are to be seen near the little settlement of "Hambleton," is supposed to have been built about 1666. It became the parish church in 1692. These ruins are now in Whitemarsh Parish. The parish church of St. Peter's Parish is now (1923) in Easton.

THE REV. MR. LILLINGSTON was minister before 1691. It is supposed that the Rev. Joseph Leich became the rector of St. Peter's Parish in 1692. Court records show that he baptized children in that section of the county as early as 1689.[4] There was a church erected at Oxford in 1695.[5] Rev. James Clayland preached in 1694, 1695 and 1696.[6]

[1] Arch. Md., Vol. 23, p. 21.
[2] Col. Oswald Tilghman in Easton "Gazette," January 7, 1914.
[3] Arch. Md., Vol. 23, p. 21.
[4] Ms. of Dr. Samuel A. Harrison.
[5] Arch. Md., Vol. 19, p. 215.
[6] Allen Ms., pp. 18–19.

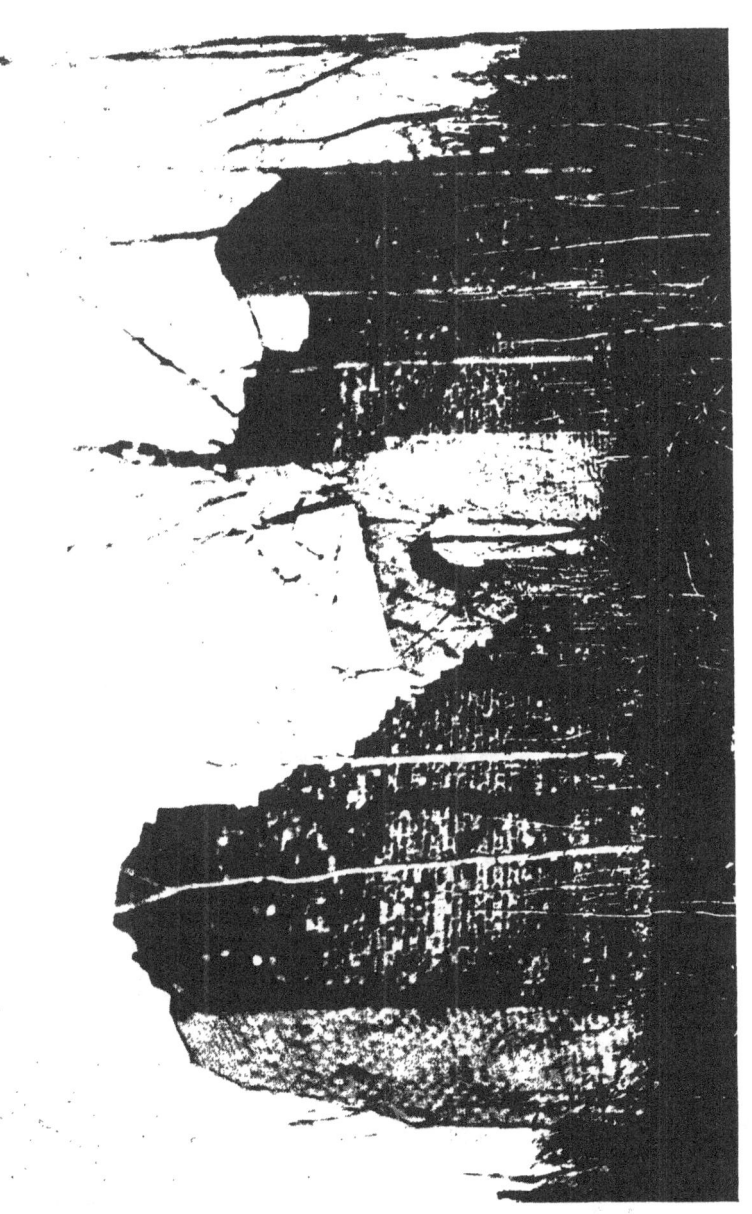

RUINS OF WHITEMARSH CHURCH
St. Peter's Parish, Talbot County

This church was built prior to the Establishment. Fell into disuse in 1858. Repaired 1896, and burned a few months thereafter.

CHRIST
St. Michael's, Talbot County

"ST. MICHAEL'S PARISH consists of Mill & Bay Hundreds and part of Island Hundred that is to say from the Court House[1] Downward."[2]

No. 22

This parish was bounded on the east by the main road that now leads from Wye Mills to Easton and by the Tred Avon river. On the south by the Choptank river. Both the Chesapeake and the Eastern bays bounded it on the west. The Wye river and Skipton creek, formerly known as Brewer's Branch, were its northern bounds.

"VESTRYMEN for the s^d Parish chosen, &^{ca} vizt
Capt John Davis
Capt James Murphy [of Rich Neck]
Mr Thomas Smithson
Mr Michaell Turbut
Mr Hugh Sherwood
Mr John Power."[3]

CHRIST CHURCH is the present representative of the original church of this old parish and stands in the town of St. Michael's.

THE REV. JAMES CLAYLAND, as minister, received in 1672 from Mr. Andrew Skinner a gift of 50 acres of land part of a grant called "Forked Neck" in Miles River Neck to be used as a Glebe "forever hereafter to be holden . . . and belonging to ye aforesaid Church of Christ there congregated."[4] He became rector of St. Michael's Parish, 1692. In 1696 he was succeeded by the Rev. Rich'd Marsden who served until 1707. The Rev. Henry Nicols was rector in 1709;[5] Rev. John Leach incumbent 1696.[6]

[1] See St. Paul's Parish (Talbot).
[2] Arch. Md., Vol. 23, p. 22.
[3] Arch. Md., Vol. 23, p. 22.
[4] Ms. of Dr. Samuel A. Harrison.
[5] Allen Ms., p. 18.
[6] B. C. Steiner in Md. Hist. Magazine, Vol. 12, p. 119.

SOMERSET COUNTY

Named after Mary Somerset, sister of Lord Baltimore.

No. 8

SOMERSET COUNTY was erected by proclamation on the 22nd of August 1666. The territory lying south of the Choptank River and extending to Watkin's Point and the line drawn from thence to the "Maine Ocean" was settled for the most part by people from the county to the south of it—the Eastern Shore of Virginia.

On February 4th, 1662, John Elzey, Randall Revell and Stephen Horsey were commissioned *Justices* for the territory. They held their offices until the 20th of the following February at which time they were reappointed, with the exception of Mr. Revell. He was succeeded by Capt. William Thorne. August 15th 1663 Capt. John Odber was added to the Justices whose names appear above.[1] They were described as "Commissioners for that part of the Province newly *seated* called the Eastern Shore." Commissions were issued on the 28th of August 1665 to Mr. Stepen Horsey and Capt. William Thorne to continue Justices on the "Eastern Shore"[2] with the following six new appointees:—George Johnson, William Stephens, John White, John Winder, James Jones, and Henry Boston, Gent. Capt. William Thorne was commissioned to command all the forces on the "Eastern Shore of the Province."

Upon the erection of Somerset county, August 22nd, 1666, the Justices who had been appointed the previous year for the "Eastern Shore," were reappointed. Mr. Stephen Horsey was made Sheriff of the new county.

---

[1] Arch. Md., Vol. 3, p. 488.
[2] Notice the fact of "Eastern Shore" being the name of the section south of the Choptank prior to 1666, at which time it became the County of Somerset.

ST. ANDREW, BUILT 1771

PRINCESS ANNE, SOMERSET COUNTY

First built as a Chapel of Ease for Somerset Parish. Now the parish church of that Parish.

St. Martin, Built About 1756
Near Berlin, Worcester County

THE FIRST PARISHES OF THE PROVINCE OF MARYLAND

"SOMERSET COUNTY was divided into Eight Hundreds, vizt
 Poquede Norton Hundred
 Mattapany   "
 Manny   "
 Pocomoke   "
 Annamessix   "
 Monakin   "
 Wiccocomoco   "
 Nantecoke   " " [1]

"SOMERSET COUNTY is divided into four Parishes, vizt
 Somerset Parish
 Coventrey "
 Stepney "
 Snow hill " " [2]

REPORT to the Assembly
 July 30 1694.
 "Somerset county has 4 Parishes laid out but never a Church."[3]

THE FIRST COURT HOUSE of Somerset County was built in 1671 at Back Creek on a part of the now well known "Westover" farm.[4] Prior to this date, as was the custom in the other counties of the Province, court was doubtless held at the home of some one of the Justices. In 1694 a court house was built near Dividing Creek. "Upon the division of the County and the erection of part of it into Worcester County, the Court House was built at Princess Anne. The present building is the third one to have been built on that spot."[5]

[1] Arch. Md., Vol. 23, p. 24.
[2] Arch. Md., Vol. 23, p. 22.
[3] Arch. Md., Vol. 20, p. 110.
[4] H. Fillmore Lankford.
[5] Hon. Joshua W. Miles

No. 23

"SOMERSET PARISH consists of Manokin and Manny hundreds."[1] The parish extended from the Wicomico river to the Manokin river.

"VESTRYMEN for the s^d Parish as by Return, vizt
Mr John Huett
Mr Richard Chambers
Mr John Panter
Mr Nathaniel Horsey
Mr Miles Grey
Mr Peter Elzey."[2]

NO CHURCH had been built but provision was made for its erection shortly after the choosing of the Vestrymen (1692). Dr. Ethan Allen states in his manuscript history of the various parishes that "All Saints Church was there before 1691." He also states that the Rev. Mr. Huett was preaching there. This church is doubtless the one now known as "Old Monie" and stands just West of Princess Anne, the county seat of Somerset County.

THE REV. GEORGE TROTTER was incumbent of this parish in 1696.[3] The Rev. Alexander Adams served as rector of the parish for 65 years—from 1704 until his death in 1769.[4]

---

[1] Arch. Md., Vol. 23, p. 22
[2] Arch. Md., Vol 23, p. 22.
[3] B. C. Steiner, Md. Hist. Magazine, Vol. 12, p. 119.
[4] Allen Ms.

ALL SAINTS
Somerset Parish, Monie, Somerset County

The first church in this parish was built prior to the Establishment. The Rev. Thomas Chase was rector of this parish at the time, April 17, 1741, that his son, Samuel Chase, was born. Samuel Chase became distinguished as a lawyer and in 1796 was nominated by President Washington a Judge of the Supreme Court of the United States.

RUINS OF REHOBOTH CHURCH
COVENTRY PARISH, SOMERSET COUNTY
This church replaced a church in which the first vestry meeting of the parish was held, 1693.

"Thou art crumbling to the dust, old pile; thou art hastening to thy fall;
And round thee, in thy loneliness, clings the ivy to the wall.
The worshippers are scattered now who knelt before thy shrine
And silence reigns where anthems rose in the days of 'Auld Lang Syne.'"
Lines written in old Blandford Church, Virginia.

THE FIRST PARISHES OF THE PROVINCE OF MARYLAND 151

No. 24
"COVENTRY PARISH consists of Pocomoke and Annamessix hundreds."[1] This parish extended from the Manokin river to the Pocomoke river.

"VESTRYMEN for the s^d Parish as by Return, vizt
Mr Francis Jenckins
Mr George Layfield
Mr Thomas Nuball
Mr William Planer S^r
Mr Thomas Dixon
Mr William Coleburn."[2]

IN THE OLD CHURCH at Rehoboth, Maryland, the vestry met in 1692, when they held their first meeting under the Act of Establishment. The ruins of the second church are to be seen today not far from Pocomoke City.

THE REV. JAMES BRECHIN was rector 1696-1698. He was succeeded by the Rev. Robert Keith in 1707.[3]

---

[1] Arch. Md., Vol. 23, p. 22.
[2] Arch. Md., Vol. 23, p. 22.
[3] Allen Ms., p. 18.

No. 25

"STEPNEY PARISH consists of Wiccocomoco & Nantecoke Hundreds."[1] The old parish was bounded on the north and west by the Nanticoke river and on the south and east by the Wicomoco river.

"VESTRYMEN for the s^d Parish as by Return, vizt
Mr James Weatherley
Mr John Bounds
Mr Philip Carter
Mr Robert Collyer
Mr Thomas Holebrooke
Mr Philip Askue."[2]

STEPNEY CHURCH commonly called "Green Hill Church," to which yearly pilgrimages are now made, was a place of worship for the settlers of the upper part of Somerset County. The present building erected 1733 has this date set in the brick of the east end. Spring Hill (Goddard's Chapel) or Quantico Church was first built (1711) as a Chapel of Ease for this Parish.[3] The present church was erected prior to the Revolutionary War.

THE REV. MR. HUETT was the officiating clergyman in 1695. The records of Somerset county show marriages performed by him in October 1682. He died 1697.[4] In 1696 Rev. George Trotter was incumbent of Stepney Parish.[5]

---

[1] Arch. Md., Vol. 23, p. 23.
[2] Arch. Md., vol. 23, p. 23.
[3] Somerset County Records I, K, L, 112.
[4] Allen Ms., p. 18.
[5] B. C. Steiner in Md. Hist. Magazine, Vol. 12, p. 119.

STEPNEY, BUILT 1733
GREEN HILL, WICOMICO COUNTY
(Stepney Parish, Somerset County, in 1692.)

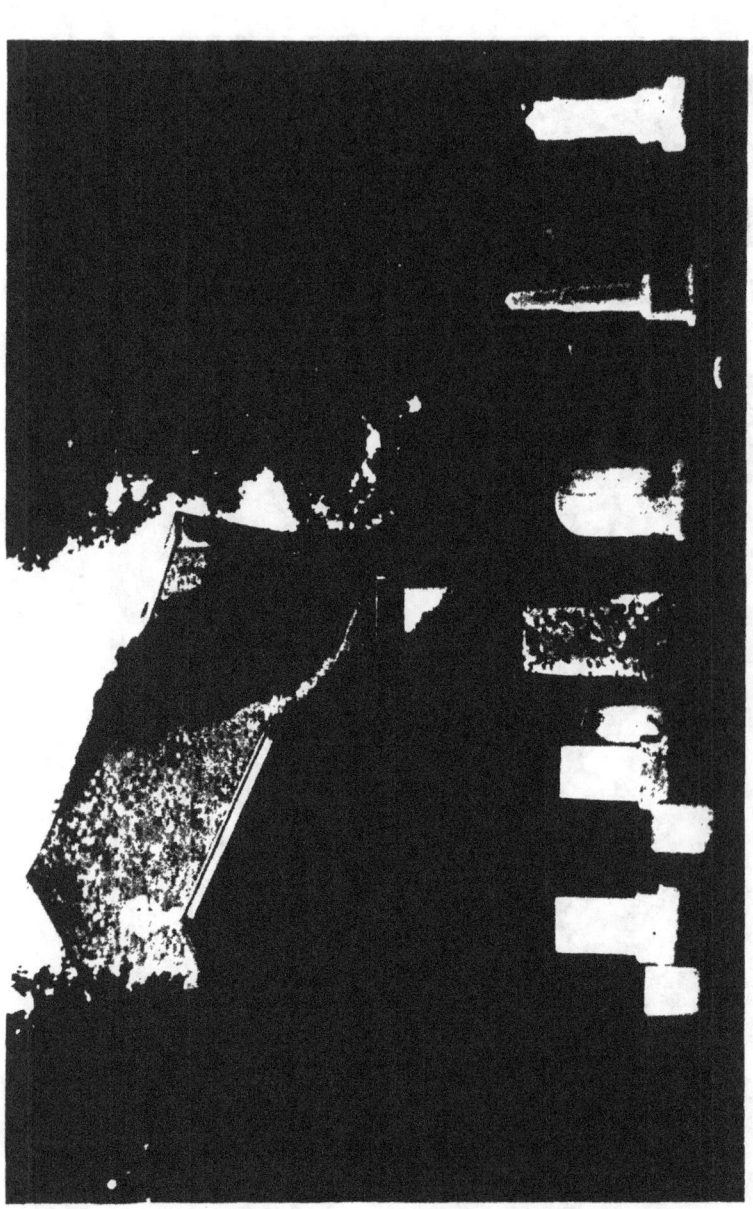

ALL HALLOWS, BUILT 1756

Snow Hill, Worcester County

This church replaced a wooden church which had served as the parish church. It stood near the banks of the Pocomoke River.

THE FIRST PARISHES OF THE PROVINCE OF MARYLAND 153

No. 26
"SNOW HILL PARISH consists of Bogettenorten & Mattapany Hundreds."[1] Also known as All Hallows Parish. This old parish extended east from the Pocomoke river to the Atlantic ocean and from the Virginia line to far within the present lines of the State of Delaware.

"VESTRYMEN for the s^d Parish as by Return, vizt
Mr Matt: Scarborough
Mr William Round
Mr John Francklin
Mr Thomas Pointer
Mr Thomas Selbey
Mr Edward Hammond."[2]

ALL HALLOWS CHURCH is the parish Church and the present building stands in Snow Hill.

THE REV. JAMES BRECHIN was incumbent 1696.[3] The Rev. Robert Keith preached at All Hallows in 1703.[4]

WORCESTER PARISH was erected out of the parish[5], by Act of Assembly 1744, Chapter 24. St. Martin is the name of parish Church.

---

[1] Arch. Md., Vol. 23, p. 23.
[2] Arch. Md., Vol. 23, p. 23.
[3] B. C. Steiner in Md. Hist. Magazine, Vol. 12, p. 119.
[4] Allen Ms., p. 18.
[5] Bacon's Laws of Maryland.

DORCHESTER COUNTY

Named for the Earl of Dorset.

No. 9
DORCHESTER COUNTY was erected in 1669. That part of the original territory called the "Eastern Shore," including the county of Somerset, that lay between the Choptank river on the north and the Nanticoke river on the south and east was the extent of the county of Dorchester. Its north-eastern limits were identical with those of the Province.

"DORCHESTER COUNTY is divided into five Hundreds, vizt

Hermitage	Hundred
Great Choptanck	"
Fishing Creek	"
Nantecoke	"
Little Choptanck	" "[1]

"AND THAT WHERE THE COURT HOUSES within any of the Counties of province are placed convenient where Churches may stand or be Erected, that in such case the said Court Houses be made use off for Churches to perform Divine Duty and Service in; especially Dorchester County Court house in the parish of Great Choptanck, so that instead of Building a Church at Cambridge, the vestrey may build a Chappell of Ease in some other convenient place."[2]

---

[1] Arch. Md., Vol. 23, p. 24.
[2] Arch. Md., Vol. 20, p. 283.

SITE OF ST. PAUL'S CHURCH
VIENNA, DORCHESTER COUNTY

First built as a Chapel of Ease for Great Choptank Parish, order for its building being issued July 8th, 1696.

THE FIRST PARISHES OF THE PROVINCE OF MARYLAND 155

"DORCHESTER COUNTY is divided into two Parishes, vizt Great Choptanck and Dorchester Parish."
"The Bounds whereof being Artificiall and some what long I have not here inserted. But are Entered among the Councill proceedings had and taken in Sr Edm^d Andros's time being then Returned but no Acco't of the Vestrymen was therein."[1]

REPORT to the Assembly
"July 30, 1694. They can Give noe certain Returne as yet for the County of Dorchester."[2]

"Wee the said Justices and Freeholders . . . did agree and consent unto that the said County of Dorchester should be Divided into two several Districts and Parishes by a Divisionale Line drawne from the Mouth of Little Choptank River binding therewith to the head of the said River from thence with a straight Line drawne to the head of the North branch of Black Water River to a plantation now in the Tenure or occupation of Benjamin Hunt of this County thence runing downe the said river on its severall Courses to the Mouth of the same. The Eastermost of which Parishes is named and called by the Name of Great Choptanck Parish, the other Parish is called and knowne by the name of Dorchester Parish . .
June 10th 1693.
         Hu. Eccleston, Cl. Com.
         Dorchester."[3]

[1] Arch. Md., Vol. 23, p. 22.
[2] Arch. Md., Vol. 20, p. 111.
[3] Arch. Md., Vol. 20, p. 67.

No. 27 GREAT CHOPTANK PARISH was on the northern side of the county and included most of the present county of Dorchester. The parish was divided from Dorchester parish on the south by a line "Begining at the mouth of the little Choptanck binding therewith to the head of s^d River,—from thence with a straight line to the north Branch of Blackwater River to Benj. Hunt's Plantation, thence down said river to the mouth of the same."[1]

"VESTRYMEN: yet do find by a Return of the Vestry of Great Choptanck Parish the s^d Return being Subscribed thus, vizt
Mr Phil V. Pitt
Mr Obadiah King
Mr Edward Stephens
Mr John Person
Mr John Lecompt."[2]

"ALSO it being represented by the Burgesses of Dorchester County that the Court house at Cambridge Stands convenient for a Church in the Parish it is built in; Ordered it be Used for that End also."[3]

"The petition of Philip Pitt and others vestrymen of the parish of Great Choptanck in Dorchester County read and thereupon the the House are of the opinion that the s^d Vestry proceed to build their church as to them shall seem convenient."[4]

THE REV. THOMAS HOWELL was the first Minister, 1696–1728 of Great Choptank Parish.[5]

ST. MARY'S WHITE CHAPEL PARISH was erected from this parish by Act of the Assembly 1725, Chapter 6.[6]

[1] Arch. Md., Assembly Proceedings 1693.
[2] Arch. Md., Vol. 23, p. 22.
[3] Arch. Md., Vol. 19, p. 234, and various authorities.
[4] Arch. Md., Vol. 19, p. 359.
[5] Allen Ms.
[6] Bacon's Laws of Maryland.

CHRIST
CAMBRIDGE, DORCHESTER COUNTY

The first services of the Church after the Establishment were held in this parish (Great Choptank) in the Court House at Cambridge.

TRINITY, SAID TO HAVE BEEN BUILT PRIOR TO THE ESTABLISHMENT

CHURCH CREEK, DORCHESTER COUNTY

Twice in its existence, in 1853 and again in 1914, this old Church has been repaired, after falling into decay and disuse, and while it may be the oldest church, it has not been continuously used as a place of worship as long as has St. Paul's Church, Kent County.

THE FIRST PARISHES OF THE PROVINCE OF MARYLAND 157

No. 28 DORCHESTER PARISH occupied all of the territory south of the Little Choptank and the line that connected it with the Black Water river. Some later writers contend that the waters of Fishing Creek are really the headwaters of the Little Choptank.

"VESTRYMEN for Dorchester parish as by Return, vizt
Mr Arthur Witley
Mr William Robison
Mr John Button
Mr Thomas Vickers
Mr James Moadsly
Mr William Shinton. [Shenton]"[1]

THE OLD CHURCH of Dorchester Parish which is still standing is said to have been built prior to the "Establishment." It is known as Trinity Church, first receiving this name April 17, 1853 when consecrated by the Rt. Rev. Henry J. Whitehouse, then Bishop of Illinois, and acting for Bishop Wm. R. Whittingham, then Bishop of Maryland, who was sick at the time.

THE REV. THOMAS HOWELL was rector from 1697 to 1708;[2] the Rev. Thomas Howell incumbent in 1696.[3] The Rev. Mr. Huett was preaching in Dorchester Parish in 1691.[4]

---

[1] Arch. Md., Vol. 23, p. 22.
[2] Allen Ms.
[3] B. C. Steiner in Md. Hist. Magazine, Vol. 12, p. 119.
[4] Allen Ms., p. 15.

CECIL COUNTY

Named after Cecilius Calvert, second Lord Baltimore.

No. 10
CECIL COUNTY was erected by proclamation in 1674. Its boundaries included, for about two weeks, all of the area now within the two counties of Cecil and Kent.

The proclamation erecting the county bore date of June 6th, 1674, and its provisions were met with such a storm of protests from the inhabitants of the lower part of what is now Kent county that the Proprietary in less than two weeks issued an "Order," June 19th 1674, giving back to Kent what she had held as hers for many years. The "Order" read in part as follows:—" . . that so much of the Eastern side as was formerly added to Kent County doe still remaine and belong to the s^d County as aforesaid—."[1]

"CECIL COUNTY is divided into two four Hundreds, vizt

Worton	Hundred
South Sassafrax	"
Bohemia	"
Elk	" "[2]

---

[1] Arch. Md., Council Proceedings 1674.
[2] Arch. Md., Vol. 23, p. 24.

TRINITY
ELKTON, CECIL COUNTY

ST. MARY, BUILT 1743
NORTHEAST, CECIL COUNTY
NORTH ELK, OR ST. MARY ANNE'S PARISH

This church succeeded one built, probably, about the time, 1706, of the laying out of the parish.

THE FIRST PARISHES OF THE PROVINCE OF MARYLAND   159

"CECIL COUNTY is divided into two Parishes, vizt
    South Sassafrax
    North Sassafrax."[1]

    These two parishes comprised all of the county and they were divided by the "Sassafrax" river.

REPORT TO THE ASSEMBLY
    July 30 1694
    "Cecil County hath 3 parishes
        1 vacant of both
        Church & Minister."[2]

THE COURT HOUSE was first located on Ordinary Point on the Sassafras River. Later on moved to Charlestown and still later to "Head of Elk," now Elkton, the present County Seat.

---

[1] Arch. Md., Vol. 23, p. 20.
[2] Arch. Md., Vol. 20, p. 111.
    The Fulham records mention 31 parishes in the province. It was evidently expected that the other parish (St. Andrew's) would be laid out to cover the territory to the north of the Elk river. Just why it never was laid out I have been unable to find. The records of the county show that only two parishes were laid out notwithstanding the "Report" to the Assembly.

"SOUTH SASSAFRAX PARISH consists of these following Hundreds, vizt
No. 29   Worton   Hundred
          South Sassafrax   "   "[1]

At that time the parish was bounded on the north by the Sassafras river, on the west by the Chesapeake Bay, on the south by a line running from the head of Worton creek to some point on Morgan's creek. Like the other border parishes its outer bounds were identical with those of the Province.[3]

"VESTRYMEN for the said Parish as by Return, vizt
    Col. William Peirce
    Mr William Harris
    Mr Edward Blay
    Mr William Elins
    Mr George Sturton
    Mr Edward Scidmore"[2]

SHREWSBURY CHURCH at the head of Turners creek in Kent County was the parish church. It was first built about 1693. The present church in 1823.

THE REV. LAWRENCE VANDERBUSH, the first rector, was serving from 1692 until his death in 1696.[3] The Rev. Rich'd Sewell succeeded him;[4] which is confirmed by another authority.[5]

---

[1] Arch. Md., Vol. 23, p. 20.
[2] Arch. Md., Vol. 23, p. 20.
[3] See St. Paul's Parish, Kent County.
[4] Allen Ms., p. 18.
[5] B. C. Steiner in Md. Hist. Magazine, Vol. 12, p. 119.

SHREWSBURY, BUILT 1832
Locust Grove, Kent County

When Shrewsbury Parish was laid out in 1692 a church, according to the records, was then standing that had been built prior to 1691. The first parish church was built in 1693, repaired in 1701, again in 1705, and rebuilt of brick in 1729. That one was torn down in 1829 and the present one built in 1832.

ST. STEPHEN
EARLEVILLE, CECIL COUNTY

When the first parish church of North Sassafras Parish was built, 1705, it succeeded a "Meeting House" which was standing as early as 1691. The parish church has been rebuilt three times: 1737, 1823 and again in 1873.

No. 30 "NORTH SASSAFRAX PARISH consists of Bohemia and Elk Hundreds."[1] It was bounded on the south by the Sassafras river on the east its bounds were the same as those of the Province. This was true of the northern boundary also. The Chesapeake bay was its western boundary. It was later called St. Stephen's Parish.

VESTRYMEN for the s^d Parish as by Return, vizt
Coll. Caspa^r Herman
Maj^r John Thompson
Mr William Ward
Mr Henry Rigg
Mr Matth. Vanderhaden
Mr Henry Jones."[2]

ST. STEPHEN'S CHURCH stands at the head of Bohemia river. The first church on the spot was begun in 1702 and dedicated in 1706.

THE REV. LAWRENCE VANDERBUSH was rector from 1692 to 1694. The Rev. Rich'd Sewell was incumbent in 1696.[5] He was sent as rector of this and South Sassafras Parish[3] in 1697. He also preached at St.Ann's Church near Middletown,[4] Delaware, about 1704.

NORTH ELK PARISH was erected[6] out of this parish by Act of the Assembly in 1706, Chapter 4. It is now called St. Mary Ann's Parish.

---

[1] Arch. Md., Vol. 23, p. 20.
[2] Arch. Md., Vol. 23, p. 21.
[3] See St. Paul's Parish Records, Kent County.
[4] Hist. of Delaware, Conrad.
[5] B. C. Steiner in Md. Hist. Magazine, Vol. 12, p. 119.
[6] Bacon's Laws of Maryland.

ST. BARNABAS, BUILT 1772
LEELAND, PRINCE GEORGE'S COUNTY

Parish Church of Queen Anne Parish, laid out 1704. In the St. Barnabas Church which preceded this building was placed over the altar a painting of the Last Supper by Gustavus Hesselius. The trusses that hold the vaulted roof have

PART VII

Papers relating to the Establishment.
Census of Maryland 1696.
Parishes of Maryland and the
District of Columbia 1922.

ST. LUKE, BUILT 1730-31

Church Hill, Queen Anne's County

It succeeded a Chapel of Ease for St. Paul's Parish which had stood on the same site as early as 1709 and was then known as the "Up River Church."

INDUCTION OF AN INCUMBENT

"The bearer hereof is M[r] Stephen Bordley who is sent by the Right Honorable and Right Reverend Father in God, Henry, Lord Bishop of London in order to officiate as a clergyman of the Church of England in this his Majesty's Province of Maryland; I do therefore, in his Majesty's name appoint the same M[r] Stephen Bordley to officiate as a clergyman of the Church of England in the Parish of S[t] Paul in Kent County.

Given under my hand and seal at the Port of Annapolis the 23rd day of June in the year of the reign of our Sovereign Lord William the Third, by the Grace of God of England, Scotland, France and Ireland, King, Defender of the Faith &[c] Anno Domini 1697.

Francis Nicholson.[1]

* * * * * * * * * * * *
*   SEAL   *
* * * * * * * * * * * *

To
   The Vestrymen of S[t] Paul's Parish, Kent County,— These."

---

[1] Governor of the Province.

At a Council Meeting at Annapolis
June 1700

There was a letter written to the Commissioners of Trade and Plantation refuting some charges made against the Law by the members of the Church of Rome and by the Quakers. The letter is in part as follows:

"We[1] assert to your Lord^{spps}, for an undoubted truth, that there is nothing imposed upon any dissenting Protestant or even Papist but the payment of 40 $^{lb.}$ p poll equal with his Maj^{ties} other Protestant Subjects & none of the other injunctions in that Law have been so much as pretended to be imposed upon any dissenting Protestant but, on the contrary they are permitted the quiet & peaceable enjoyment & use of their Religion wth out the Least Molestation whatsoever & therefore they greatly wrong that Law & the Gov^t by their Insinuations in the first second & third exceptions.

There has no sects of Religion here opposed that law but the Papists and the Quakers who from the first beginning of his Maties happy Gov^t here with which that Law entered, have with their greatest might obstructed it, . . . in fine may it please your Lordships their design is not only against that Law but Extablishing Protestant Religion here, and there might be no more Countenance given to it now under his Maties Gov^t than was under Lord Baltimore's who was a Papist & as they say so it was Liberty of Conscience to all without publick Countenance to any but we are assured as by his Maties matchless valour and conduct he pre-

---
1. Members of the Provincial Council

served our lives and fortunes from destruction no less our Religion also and we hope to enjoy both and at the same time permit the Quiet Exercise of Dissenters in theirs while they will use it with peace and quietness. With which we will beg your Lord^{sps} pardon for so intruding so long upon your patience and beg leave to subscribe

    Your Lordships most humble &
      Obedient Serv^{ts}
      Hen: Jowles
      Jno. Addison
      Tho. Brooke
      Tho. Tasker
      Jno. Hammond"

CENSUS OF THE PROVINCE IN 1696[1]

"Countys	Parishes	Tithables	Tobacco	Incumbents
St. Mary's	William and Mary	532	21,280	Benj. Nobbs
St. Mary's	King and Queen	473	18,920	Chris Platts
Calvert	Christ Church	537	21,480	Hugh Jones
Calvert	All Saints'	507	20,280	Tho. Cockshutt
Prince George	All Faiths'	278	11,120	————
Prince George	St. Paul's	500	20,000	Monsieur Morien
Prince George	Piscattaway	—	—	
Charles	William and Mary	258	10,320	————
Charles	Port Tobacco	—	—	————
Charles	Manjemy	175	19,000	George Tubman
Anne Arundel	Herring Creek	507	20,280	Henry Hall
Anne Arundel	South River	460	18,400	Tho. Clayton
Anne Arundel	Middle Neck	374	14,960	Peregrine Coney
(Port Annapolis is in Middle Neck)				
Anne Arundel	Broad Neck	223	8,920 ⎫	Edw'd Topp, Jr.
Baltimore	Patapsco	218	8,720 ⎭	
Baltimore	St. John's	128	5,120	————
Baltimore	St. George's	137	5,480	————
Cecil	South Sassafras	350	14,000 ⎫	Rich'd Sewell
Cecil	North Sassafras	321	12,840 ⎭	
Kent	Kent Island	146	5,840	————
Kent	St. Paul	338(?)	15,320	Stephen Bordley
Talbot	St. Paul's	606	24,240	John Lillingston
Talbot	St. Peter's	453	18,120	————
Talbot	St. Michael's	485	19,400	—— Leach
Dorchester	Choptank	407	16,280 ⎫	Tho. Howell
Dorchester	Dorchester	221	8,840 ⎭	
Somersett	Somersett	304	12,160	Geo. Trotter
Somersett	Coventry	369	14,760	————
Somersett	Stepney	362	14,480	Geo. Trotter ut supra
Somersett	Snow Hill	356	14,240	James Brechin"

---

[1] B. C. Steiner, "Some Unpublished Manuscripts from Fulham Palace Relating to Provincial Maryland." Maryland Historical Magazine, Vol. XII, p. 118-119.

THE FIRST PARISHES OF THE PROVINCE OF MARYLAND 171

ACTS OF THE ASSEMBLY
Subsequent to the Establishment

1698.	Chapter 5.	Division line between St. Paul's and Shrewsbury Parishes.
1699.	Chpater 50.	Providing for Church (St. Ann's) Middle Neck Parish, Anne Arundel County.
1700.	Chapter 5.	Land given to Christ Church Parish, Calvert County.
1701.	Chapter 5.	Land for St. James Herring Creek Parish, Anne Arundel County.
1704.	Chapter 96.	Queen Anne Parish erected from St. Paul's Parish, Prince George County.
1706.	Chapter 4.	North Elk Parish erected in Cecil County.
1706.	Chapter 7.	Newport Hundred taken from King and Queen Parish and added to William and Mary Parish, Charles County.
1718.	Chapter 8.	Providing for church, St. Ann's, Middle Neck Parish, Anne Arundel County.
1719.	Chapter 6.	Rector of St. John's Parish, given "Stoakley Manor," Baltimore County.
1720.	Chapter 4.	Old State House and lot at St. Mary's City "settled on" Rector of William and Mary Parish, St. Mary's County.
1722.	Chapter 3.	Part of St. Paul's Parish, Baltimore County, annexed to Westminster Parish, Anne Arundel County.
1725.	Chapter 9.	Chapel of Ease at Vienna, Great Choptank Parish, Dorchester County.
1725.	Chapter 10.	St. Mary's White Chapel Parish erected out of Great Choptank Parish, Dorchester County.
1726.	Chapter 6.	Prince George's Parish erected out of St. John's Parish (Piscattaway), Prince George's County.
1727.	Chapter 10.	Providing Parish Church, St. Paul's Parish, Baltimore County.
1728.	Chapter 19.	St. Luke's Parish erected out of St. Paul's Parish, Queen Anne's County.
1728.	Chapter 15.	Queen Caroline Parish erected, Anne Arundel County.
1728.	Chapter 25.	Chapel of Ease, Middle Neck Parish, Anne Arundel County.
1729.	Chapter 11.	Chapel of Ease, Middle Neck Parish, Anne Arundel County.
1729.	Chapter 10.	New Church, All Hallow's Parish, Anne Arundel County.
1729.	Chapter 13.	Erecting church, St. Luke's Parish, Queen Anne County.
1730.	Chapter 2.	Chapel of Ease at Vienna, Great Choptank Parish, Dorchester County.
1730.	Chapter 9.	Church, St. Paul's Parish, Baltimore County.
1731.	Chapter 4.	New Church, Westminster Parish, Anne Arundel County.
1731.	Chapter 11.	Church, St. Paul's Parish, Baltimore County.
1732.	Chapter 12.	New Church, Christ Church Parish, Calvert County.
1732.	Chapter 28.	New Church, Durham Parish, Charles County.
1732.	Chapter 29.	New Church and Chapel of Ease, St. Paul's Parish, Prince George's County.

172 THE FIRST PARISHES OF THE PROVINCE OF MARYLAND

ACTS OF ASSEMBLY—Continued

1733.	Chapter 10.	New Church and Chapel of Ease, North Sassafras Parish, Cecil County.
1735.	Chapter 9.	New church to be built and Newport Church repaired, King and Queen Parish, St. Mary's County.
1736.	Chapter 12.	Church in Durham Parish, Charles County.
1736.	Chapter 13.	Same as Chapter 9, 1735.
1737.	Chapter 5.	Same as Chapter 10, 1733.
1742.	Chapter 9.	St. Mary Ann's Parish erected, Cecil County.
1742.	Chapter 15.	St. Thomas' Parish erected, Baltimore County.
1742.	Chapter 18.	All Saint's Parish erected, Frederick County.
1744.	Chapter 3.	Augustine Parish erected, Cecil County.
1744.	Chapter 14.	Trinity Parish erected, Charles County.
1744.	Chapter 14.	St. Mary's County divided into four parishes.
1744.	Chapter 26.	Chapel of Ease erected on land given by Wm. Scott, (————?) County.
1744.	Chapter 2.	Chapel already built to be made a Chapel of Ease, Prince George's Parish.
1744.	Chapter 21.	Land for St. James Herring Creek Parish, Anne Arundel County.
1744.	Chapter 24.	Worcester Parished erected, Worcester County.
1745.	Chapter 4.	Same as Chapter 14, 1744.
1746.	Chapter 8.	Chapel of Ease to be built, Christ Church Parish, Calvert County.
1747.	Chapter 9.	Church and two chapels of ease to be built in All Saints Parish, Frederick County.
1747.	Chapter 18.	Land. Westminster Parish, Anne Arundel County.
1747.	Chapter 24.	Land. Middle Neck Parish, Anne Arundel County.
1748.	Chapter 2.	Chapel of Ease, Shrewsbury Parish, Kent County.
1748.	Chapter 4.	Bounds of King and Queen Parish, St. Mary's County.
1748.	Chapter 4.	Bounds of All Faith Parish, St. Mary's County.
1748.	Chapter 4.	Same as Chapter 14, 1744, St. Mary's County.
1748.	Chapter 6.	New church at Snow Hill, Worcester County.
1748.	Chapter 8.	Church enlarged, Christ Church Parish, Kent Island.
1748.	Chapter 9.	Trinity Parish, Charles County.
1748.	Chapter 9.	Bounds of King and Queen Parish, St. Mary's County.
1748.	Chapter 13.	St. John's Parish erected, Queen Anne County.
1748.	Chapter 16.	Chapel of Ease, St. John's Parish, Baltimore County.
1749.	Chapter 6.	Parish Church, St. Paul's Parish, Baltimore County.
1750.	Chapter 7.	New Church and Chapel of Ease, St. George's Parish, Baltimore, now Harford County.
1750.	Chapter 8.	Parish Church to be enlarged, William and Mary Parish, St. Mary's County.
1750.	Chapter 21.	Parish Church, All Saints Parish, Frederick County.
1750.	Chapter 21.	Chapel of Ease to be erected, King and Queen Parish, St. Mary's County.

THE FIRST PARISHES OF THE PROVINCE OF MARYLAND 173

ACTS OF ASSEMBLY—Concluded

1751.	Chapter 6.	Glebe, Durham Parish, Charles County.
1751.	Chapter 9.	Parish Church and Chapel of Ease to be built in Trinity Parish, Charles County.
1751.	Chapter 12.	New church to be built, Portobacco Parish, Charles County.
1751.	Chapter 23.	Chapel of Ease to be built, Coventry Parish, Somerset County.
1752.	Chapter 6.	Parish Church and Chapel of Ease.
1753.	Chapter 12.	Same as Chapter 12, 1751.
1753.	Chapter 18.	Chapel of Ease repaired, St. Paul's Parish, Prince Georges County.
1753.	Chapter 19.	Vestrymen, St. Andrews Parish, St. Mary's County.
1754.	Chapter 6.	Chaptico Church to be repaired, King and Queen Parish, St. Mary's County.
1754.	Chapter 7.	Chapel of Ease at Ivy Springs, Portobacco Parish, Charles County.
1755.	Chapter 14.	Chapel of Ease, Worcester Parish, Worcester County.
1755.	Chapter 15.	New Church, St. Mary's White Chapel Parish, Dorchester County.
1756.	Chapter 7.	Same as Chapter 6, 1748, Worcester County.
1757.	Chapter 18.	Same as Chapter 7, 1750, Baltimore County.
1758.	Chapter 2.	Same as Chapter 7, 1750, Baltimore County.
1762.	Chapter 16.	Chapel. Somerset Parish, Somerset County.
1762.	Chapter 25.	Chapel of Ease to be built at T. L., St. Paul's Parish, Baltimore County.
1762.	Chapter 28.	New Church to be built St. James Herring Creek Parish, Anne Arundel County.
1763.	Chapter 14.	Relating to No. Sassafras, Parish, Cecil County.
1763.	Chapter 27.	Enlarging Church, St. Johns Parish, Baltimore County.
1765.	Chapter 32.	Chester Parish erected, Kent County.
1770.	Chapter 18.	St. James Parish erected, Baltimore County.
1770.	Chapter 9.	Eden alias Zion Parish erected, Frederick County.
1770.		St. John's Parish, Hagerstown, erected Frederick County.

BALTIMORE CITY
CATHEDRAL OF THE INCARNATION

Churches In Use 1923

Advent
All Saints'
Ascension
Christ
Christ Church Chapel
Emanuel
Epiphany, Govans
Grace and St. Peter
Grace Deaf Mute Mission
Grace Chapel, Mt. Winans
Guardian Angel
Holy Cross
Holy Comforter
Holy Evangelist
Holy Innocents
Holy Nativity
Holy Trinity
Messiah
Memorial
Mt. Calvary
Nativity, Cedarcroft
Our Savior
Prince of Peace
Redeemer, Govans

Redemption
St. Andrew's
St. Andrew's, Hamilton
St. Bartholomew's
St. David's, Roland Park
St. James', Irvington
St. James' (Colored)
St. John's
St. John's, Catonsville Ave.
St. John's, Mt. Washington
St. Katharine's Chapel
St. Luke's
St. Margaret's
St. Mary the Virgin Chapel
   (Colored)
St. Mary's, Hampden
St. Michael and All Angels
St. Mathias, Belgravia
St. Paul's
St. Paul's Chapel
St. Philip's, Highlandtown
St. Stephen the Martyr
St. Thomas', Homestead
Trinity, Ten Hills

DISTRICT OF COLUMBIA
CATHEDRAL OF ST. PETER AND ST. PAUL
(The National Cathedral)

Churches In Use 1923

Advent
All Saints'
All Souls'
Ascension
Atonement
Bethlehem Chapel
Calvary
Christ, Georgetown
Christ
Emmanuel
Esther Memorial
Epiphany
Epiphany Chapel
Good Shepherd Chapel
Grace, Georgetown
Grace
Holy Comforter Chapel
Incarnation
Nativity Chapel
Our Savior
Redeemer
Resurrection Chapel
St. Alban
St. Agnes' Chapel
St. Andrew
St. Barnabas' Chapel
St. Columba's Chapel
St. David Chapel
St. Elizabeth
St. George's Chapel
St. James'
St. John's
St. John's, Georgetown
St. John's Chapel
St. Luke's
St. Mark's
St. Margaret's
St. Mary's Chapel
St. Matthew's Chapel
St. Matthew's, Bennings
St. Matthew's, Seat Pleasant
St. Michael and All Angels
St. Monica's Chapel
St. Patrick's Chapel
St. Paul's
St. Peter and St. Paul's
St. Philip the Evangelist
St. Stephen's
St. Thomas'
Transfiguration Chapel
Trinity
Trinity, Takoma Park

MARYLAND PARISHES
E, Easton; M, Maryland; W, Washington

Advent	1900	W.	Washington, D. C.
Addison	1811	W.	Seat Pleasant
All Faith's	1692	W.	Mechanicsville
All Hallow's	1692	M.	Davidsonville
All Hallow's	1692	E.	Snow Hill
All Saint's	1875	E.	Longwoods
All Saint's	1692	M.	Sunderland
All Saint's	1742	M.	Frederick
All Saint's	1893	W.	Oakley
All Soul's	1913	W.	Washington, D. C.
Anacostia	1869	W.	Washington, D. C.
Ascension	1845	W.	Washington, D. C.
Ascension	1844	M.	Westminster
Antietam	1899	M.	Sharpsburg
Augustine	1744	E.	Chesapeake City
Brookland	1897	W.	Washington, D. C.
Catoctin	1855	M.	Thurmont
Christ Church	1818	W.	Washington, D. C.
Christ Church	1692	E.	Stevensville
Christ Church	1692	M.	Port Republic
Christ Church	1913	W.	Kensington
Chester	1765	E.	Chestertown
Churchville	1869	M.	Churchville
Congress Heights	1908	W.	Washington, D. C.
Coventry	1692	E.	Upper Fairmount
Deer Creek	1859	M.	Darlington
Durham	1692	W.	Nanjemoy
Dorchester	1692	E.	Church Creek
Emanuel	1803	M.	Cumberland
Epiphany	1871	W.	Forestville
Epiphany	1844	W.	Washington, D. C.
Georgetown	1809	W.	Georgetown
Great Choptank	1692	E.	Cambridge
Grace	1866	W.	Washington, D. C.
Grace Church	1852	W.	Washington, D. C.
Havre de Grace	1809	M.	Havre de Grace
Holy Trinity	1844	M.	Eldersburg
Holy Trinity	1844	W.	Collington
Holy Trinity		E.	Greensboro
Holy Trinity	1852	E.	Oxford
"I. U." Christ Church	1862?	E.	Worton.
Immanuel	1876	M.	Glencoe
Incarnation	1868	W.	Washington, D. C.

MARYLAND PARISHES—Continued

E, Easton; M, Maryland; W, Washington

King and Queen	1692	W.	Chaptico
Linganore	1889	M.	New Market
Miles River		E.	Tunis
North Elk	1706	E.	North East
North Sassafras	1692	E.	Earlville
North Kent	1855	E.	Massey's
Norwood	1895	W.	Bethesda
Piscattaway	Broad Creek 1692	W.	Oxonhill
Pocomoke	1855	E.	Pocomoke City
Port Tobacco	1692	W.	La Plata
Prince George	1726	W.	Rockville
Queen Anne's	1704	W.	Leeland
Queen Caroline	1728	M.	Guilford
Reisterstown	1871	M.	Reisterstown
Rock Creek	1726–1811	W.	D. C.
St. Alban's	1855	W.	Washington, D. C.
St. Andrew's	1744	W.	Leonardtown
St. Andrew's	1858	W.	Washington, D. C.
St. Ann's	1692	M.	Annapolis
St. Bartholomew's	1812	W.	Laytonsville
St. Bartholomew's		E.	Crisfield
St. George's	1692	M.	Perrymans
St. George's	1875	M.	Mt. Savage
St. James'	1770	M.	Monkton
St. James'	1873	W.	Washington, D. C.
St. James'	1692	M.	Herring Creek
St. John's	1823	W.	Accokeek
St. John's	1748	E.	Hillsboro
St. John's	1692	M.	Upper Falls
St. John's	1896	M.	Frostburg
St. John's	1700	M.	Hagerstown
St. John's	1816	W.	Washington, D. C.
St. Luke's	1728	E.	Church Hill
St. Mary Anne's	1742	E.	North East
St. Mary's Whitechapel	1725	E.	Denton
St. Mary's	1851	W.	St. Mary's City
St. Mark's	1800	M.	Petersville
St. Mark's	1869	W.	Washington, D. C.
St. Margaret's	1897	W.	Washington, D. C.
St. Matthew's	1916	M.	Sparrows Point
St. Matthew's	1811	W.	Hyattsville
St. Matthew's	1874	M.	Oakland
St. Michael's	1692	E.	St. Michael's
St. Michael's and All Angels	1893	W.	Washington, D. C.

THE FIRST PARISHES OF THE PROVINCE OF MARYLAND 179

MARYLAND PARISHES—Concluded
E, Easton; M, Maryland; W, Washington

St. Paul's	1692	E.	Fairlee
St. Paul's	1868	W.	Washington, D. C.
St. Paul's	1836	E.	Vienna
St. Paul's	1692	W.	Baden
St. Paul's	1692	E.	Centerville
St. Paul's	1692	M.	Baltimore City
St. Paul's	1842	M.	Prince Frederick
St. Paul's	1841	M.	Point of Rocks
St. Peter's	1869	M.	Patuxent Forge
St. Peter's	1792	W.	Poolesville
St. Peter's	1692	E.	Easton
St. Philip's	1848	W.	Laurel
St. Stephen's	1836	E.	East New Market
St. Stephen's	1892	W.	Washington, D. C.
St. Thomas'	1891	W.	Washington, D. C.
St. Thomas'	1891	M.	Hancock
St. Thomas'	1742	M.	Owings Mills
St. Thomas'	1851	W.	Croome
Salisbury	1848	E.	Salisbury
Severn	1838	M.	Millersville
Shrewsbury	1692	E.	Kennedyville
Sherwood	1859	M.	Cockeysville
Silver Spring	1864	W.	Woodside
Somerset	1692	E.	Princess Anne
Spring Hill	1827	E.	Quantico
Stepney	1692	E.	Bivalve
Susquehanna	1913	E.	Port Deposit
Takoma	1896	W.	Takoma Park
Trinity	1827	W.	Washington, D. C.
Trinity	1744	W.	Newport
Trinity	1869	M.	Dorsey
Trinity		E.	Elkton
Vienna	1836	E.	Vienna
Washington	1794	W.	Washington, D. C.
Western Run	1845	M.	Glyndon
Westminster	1692	M.	St. Margaret's
Whitemarsh	1858	E.	Trappe
William and Mary	1692	W.	Wayside
William and Mary	1692	W.	Valley Lee
Wicomico	1845	E.	Mt. Vernon
Worcester	1744	E.	Berlin
Wye	1860	E.	Queenstown
Zion	1811	W.	Beltsville
Zion	1804	M.	Urbana

SOURCES

McMahon's "History of Maryland."
Chalmer's "Political Annals."
Chalmer's "Opinions of Eminent Lawyers."
Henning's "Statutes at Large."
Encyclopedia Britannia, 9th Edition.
Johnson's "Founders of Maryland."
Hall's "Narratives of Early Maryland."
Archives of Maryland.
Hawk's "Ecclesiastical History of the United States," Vol. 2.
Kilty's "Landholders' Assistant."
Reports of the American Historical Society.
Thomas' "Chronicles of Colonial Maryland."
Allen's Manuscript "History of the Church in Maryland."
Baldwin's "Calendar of Wills."
Ridgely's "Old Brick Churches."
Gambrall's "Church Life in Colonial Maryland."
Mathews' "Counties of Maryland."
Bacon's "Laws of Maryland."
Scharf's "History of Baltimore County."
Tilghman's "History of Talbot County."
Earle & Skirven's "Marylands Colonial Eastern Shore."
Harrison's Manuscript "History of the Church in Talbot County."
Conrad's "History of Delaware."
Bozman's "History of Maryland."
Steiner. "Some Unpublished Manuscripts from Fulham Palace, etc."
Parish Records of the Thirty Original Parishes.
Court Records of the Ten Original Countys.
Land Records of the Ten Original Countys.
Calvert Papers.
Wroth. "The First Sixty Years of the Church of England in Maryland."

INDEX

Names, Counties, Court Houses, Hundreds, Parishes, Churches, Geographical Names and Miscellaneous.

INDEX

NAME	
Abbett, Samuel Senr.	146
Adams, Rev. Alexander	150
Richard	141
Addison, Col. John	37, 39, 40, 73, 74, 98, 135, 164
Alfred the Great	105
Allen, Rev. Ethan	106, 130
Andros, Gov. Edmund	155
Anne, Queen of England	95, 102
Arundel, Lady Anne	118
Archbishop of Canterbury	26, 28, 105
Ashman, George	40, 140
Askue, Charles	129
Philip	152
Baleter, Edward	96
Baltimore, Lord, First	3, 4, 7, 143
Second	1–11, 27, 118, 137, 148, 158
Third	14, 23, 27, 28, 29, 30, 31, 32, 130, 163
Fourth	14
Fifth	14
Barecraft, John	113
Barton, William	128, 133
Beale, Ninian	39
Thomas	112
Bennett, John	123
Bigger, John	41
Biggs, Seth	120
Bishop of Illinois	157
Bishop of London, Wm. Laud	2
Henry Compton	13, 15, 17, 18, 28, 38, 127, 145, 162
Bishop of Maryland	157
Blackiston (or Blackistone), Govr. Nathaniel	19, 72, 98
Col. Nehemiah	37, 39, 40, 113
Bladen, William	96, 101
Bland, Thomas	122
Blay, Edward	160
Boothby, Edward	40
Bordley, Rev. Stephen	117, 162
Boston, Henry	96
Bounds, John	152
Bowdle, Thomas	146

NAME	
Bozman, John	43
Bray, Rev. Thomas	18, 19, 71, 73, 74, 126
Brooke (or Brooks), Thomas	37, 40, 73, 74, 98, 128, 164
Dr. John	39, 47
Browne, Col. David	37, 39, 40
Brown, William	122
Brechin, Rev. James	153, 171
Brisco, Phillip	113
Bullett, Joseph	133, 134
Burgess, Edward	121
Button, John	157
Calverts, the	14
Calvert, Benedict	14
Cecelius	4, 5, 6, 7, 8, 10, 12, 27, 104, 111, 158
Charles	14, 27, 130
George	2, 3, 5, 143
Leonard	5, 6, 7, 8
Campbell, John	112
Canterbury, Archbishop of	26, 28, 105
Carlisle, Earl of	23
Carolina, Lords Proprietors of	23
Carter, Philip	152
Carteret, Sir George	23
Carvel, Major John	40
Chairs, John	145
Chambers, Richard	150
Charles I. of England	3, 9
Charlet, Richard	128
Chase, Samuel	97
Cheseldyne, Kenelm	39, 40, 112
Clarke, Philip	40
Clayland, Rev. James	42, 106, 146, 147
Clegate, Thomas	126
Cleybourne, William	2, 116
Clouds, Richard	113
Cockshutt, Rev. Thomas	96, 127
Codd, Col. St. Leger	41, 42
Colebatch, Rev. Joseph	121
Coleburn, William	151
Collyer, Robert	152
Commissioners of Trade & Plantation	17, 23, 30, 32, 71, 72, 74, 163

INDEX

NAME	
Conner, Philip	116
Cony, Rev. Peregrine	122
Coode, Capt. John	39, 98, 113
Copley, Govr. Lionel	14, 15, 16, 17, 37, 40, 47, 49, 58
Coppage, John	116
Corban, Nicholas	140
Cordey, Thomas	142
Cornwallis, Thomas	7
Coursey, William	145
Courtes (or Coates), Col. John	37, 39, 40, 73, 98, 132, 133
Craven, Earl of	23
Crawford, Rev. Mr.	112
Cressey, Samuel	132, 133
Cromwell, Oliver	9
Richard	139, 140
Crooke, Robert	42
Dalrumple, William	96
Dare, William	41, 42, 34
Davies (or Dawes), Rev. Thomas	106, 112, 113, 128, 129, 142
Davis, Capt. John	147
Dent, Capt. John	73, 113
William	41, 60, 134
Denton, Henry	41, 44, 49, 58, 59
Dixon, Thomas	151
Dorset, Earl of	154
Dorsey, John	41
Draper, Lawrence	122
Dulaney, Daniel	97
Eager, George	123
Eagle, Robert	123
Eareckson, Matthew	107
Eaton, Rev. Jeremiah	142
Eccleston, Hugh	155
Edmondson, John	39, 40, 41, 43
Edwards, Rev. John	141, 142
Elins, William	160
Elzey, John	148
Peter	150
Emmet, John	135
Ennals, Thomas	41, 43
Evans, Rev. Evan	142
Evernden, Thomas	41

NAME	
Ferry, John	140
Firnley, Henry	126
Finney, William	40, 145
Fowke, Elizabeth	134
Gerrard	134
Francklin, John	153
Frisby, James	37, 40
William	117
Fuller, Edward	123
Gardner, Capt. Richard	129
Gassaway, Nicholas	39
Gay, John	140
Geddes, Andrew	127
George I. of England	14
Gerrard, Capt. Thomas	102
Gillam, John	129
Godwin (or Godden), John	41
Gourwin, Thomas	13
Greenbury, Col. Nicholas	37, 39, 40
Greenfield, Thomas	41, 128
Gresham, John	121
Grey, Miles	150
Groome, Moses	141
Guilford, Lord	15
Haley, Thomas	141
Hall, Rev. Henry	120, 126, 127
Joseph	96
Hammond, Edward	153
John	41, 73, 164
Hance, John	127
Hanslope, Capt. Henry	121
Hanson, Hans	40, 117
John	133
Harbert, William	132
Hardy, Henry	132
Harness, Jacob	122
Harris, James	108
William	39, 40, 160
Harrison, Richard	133
Hatton, William	135
Hawkins, Henry	41, 133
John	133
Hawton, William	132
Heigh, James	96
Hemsley, William Jr.	144

INDEX

NAME	
Herman, Col. Casparus	161
Hill, Rev. Richard	126
Hodge, Thomas	141
Holdsworth, Samuel	126
Holebroke, Thomas	152
Hollace, William	142
Holland, Capt. William	98, 120
Hollyday, Mr. James	97
Thomas	128
Hopkins, Jonathan	144, 145
William	123
Horsey, Nathaniel	150
Stephen	148
Hoskins, Capt. Philip	41, 133, 134
Howard, Cornelius	122
Howell, Rev. Thos	156, 157
Huett (Hewett), Rev. John	40, 42, 106, 150, 152, 157
Hull, Rev. Richard	127
Hunt, Benjamin	156
Hussey, Thomas	131
Hutchins, Col. Charles	37, 40
Hutchinson, William	135
Illinois, Bishop of	157
James I. of England	3, 12
James, Charles	39
Edward	116
Rev. Richard	2, 6, 13, 116
Jenckins, Francis	151
Johnson, George	148
Jones, Edward	39, 41
Henry	161
James	148
Jowles, Col. Henry	37, 39, 40, 164
Judwin, John	146
Keech, James	129
Keith, Rev. Robert	153
Kemp, Thomas	127
King, Elias	40
Obediah	156
Robert	39
Langworth, Mr	98, 113
Laurence, Col. Wm	116

NAME	
Lawrence, Sir Thomas	37, 40
Layfield, George	151
Lecompt, John	156
Leich (or Leach), John Jr.	127
Rev. Joseph	146, 160
Lewis, Wm	7
Lillingston, Rev. John	106, 145, 146
Llewellen, John	40, 49, 58, 59, 112
Lloyd, Edward	73, 98
Lockwood, Capt. Robert	120
Lomax, C	133
Lowe, Nicholas	146
Macklin, Robert	145
Magruder, Samuel	128
Magruther, Samuel	128
Manning, John	126
Joseph	134
Marsden, Rev. Richard	147
Martin, Thomas	146
Maryland, Bishop of	157
Mary, Queen of England	35, 49, 58
Mary, the Blessed Virgin	110
Mason, Robert	40, 112
Mathews, Roger	142
Mattox, Lawrence	43
Maulden, Francis	126
Maxwell, Lt. Col	139
Merrican, Hugh	123
Miller, Michael	39, 117
Mitchell, Henry	41
Moadsly, James	157
Moore, Rev. Mr	106, 132, 133
Morien, Rev. Mr	128
Mullett, Rev. William	13, 126
Murphey, Capt. James	147
Nichols, William	127
Nicholson, Gov. Francis	17, 18, 63, 122, 162
Nicols, Rev. Henry	147
Nobbes, Rev. Benj	112
Nuball, Thomas	151
Odber, Capt. John	148
Ormond, Duke of	23
Owen, Rev. Robert	128

INDEX

NAME	
Paca, William	97
Panter, John	150
Parker, John	142
Pead, Rev. Duell	13, 121
Pearce (or Pierce), Capt. William	160
Perrett, Nicholas	120
Person, John	156
Phelps, Walter	121
Phinney (Finney?), Wm	40
Pinder, Edward	41
Pitt, Philip V	156
Planer, Wm. Sr	151
Plater, George	60
Platts, Rev. Christopher	113
Pointer, Thomas	153
Pope, The	7
Povey, John	95
Power, John	147
Preston, Capt. Thos	141
Revell, Randall	148
Richardson, Lawrence	141
Ridgeley, Henry	41
Rigbey, James	120
Rigg, Henry	161
Robins, George	146
Thomas	43, 146
Robison, William	157
Robotham, Charles	37
Col. George	39, 40
Roper, William	121
Round, William	153
Sampson, Richard	140
Sanders, James	41
Saunders, James	98
Scarborough, Matt	153
Scidmore, Edward	160
Scott, Daniel	141
John	127
Selbey, Thomas	153
Sewell, Rev. Richard	160, 161
Seymour, Govr. Joseph	102
Sherwood, Hugh	40, 147
Shinton, William	157
Siclemore, Samuel	141
Skinner, Andrew	147

NAME	
Slye, Capt. Gerrard	102
Smallwood, John	135
Major James	41
Smith, George	142
John	129
Richard	126
Robert	40
Walter	127
Smithson, Thomas	147
Smyth, Thomas	117
Somerset, Mary	148
Southern, Richard	129
Valentine	116
Sourton, Rev. Francis	13
Staley, Thomas	39, 40, 141
Stephens, Edward	156
William	148
Stoddart, James	135
Stone, John	134
William	134
Govr. William	9
Sturton, George	160
Talbot, Grace	143
Tanneyhill, Wm	135
Tasker, Thomas	41, 127, 164
Taylard, W	44, 94, 101
Tayler, Abraham	141
Lawrence	142
Tench, Thomas	37, 40, 120
Theakston, Thomas	42
Theodore of Tarsus	105
Thomas, John	39
Major John	140
Thompson, Major John	161
Thorne, Capt. Wm	148
Tilden, Charles	117
Tilley, Joseph	120
Topp, Rev. Edw. Jr	123, 140
Trippe, Major Henry	39, 41
Trotter, Rev. George	150, 152
Tubman, Rev. George	132, 133, 134, 135
Turbut, Michael	147
Turling, Rev. John	106, 126, 128, 129, 134
Turner, Wm	127

INDEX

NAME

Vanderbush, Rev. Lawrence 106, 117, 160, 161
Vanderhaden, Matthew........ 161
Vickers, Thomas.............. 157

Walkers, Alexander............ 116
Ward, William................ 161
Warner, George..........34, 41, 42
Watkings (or Watkins), Francis 40, 140
Watkins, John.............100, 121
Watson, John...............40, 112
Weatherly, James............. 152
Wharfield, Richard............ 122
Wheeler, Samuel.............. 40
White, John.................. 148
Whitehouse, Rt. Rev. Henry J.. 157
Whittingham, Rt. Rev. Wm. R.. 157

NAME

Whittington, John............. 145
    William.........40, 43
Wielder, John................. 132
Wilkinson, Rev. William.....6, 9, 13
William III. of England...14, 35, 49, 58, 93, 94, 97, 162
Williamson, "Mr. Secretary"... 23
Wilmore, Simon............... 117
Winder, John................. 148
Witley, Arthur................ 157
Woolford, Roger............... 43
Wootton, Rev. James.......122, 123
Workman, Anthony............ 116
Wright, Nathaniel............. 145
Wroth, James................. 42
Wynne, Edward............... 40

Yates, Robert................. 132
Yeo, Rev. John..... 13, 26, 141, 142

INDEX

HUNDREDS	OLD COUNTY	
Annemessex	Somerset	149, 151
Bay	Talbot	143, 147
Bohemia	Cecil	158, 161
Broad Neck	Anne Arundel	119, 123
Bollingbroke	Talbot	143, 146
Chaptico	St. Mary's	110
Chester River, Lower	Kent	115
Upper	Kent	115
Chester	Talbot	143
Choptank, Great	Dorchester	154
Little	Dorchester	154
Cliffs, Lower End of	Calvert	124, 126
Upper End of	Calvert	124, 127
Eastern Neck	Kent	115
Elk	Cecil	158, 161
Elkton Head	Calvert	124, 126
Fishing Creek	Dorchester	154
Gunpowder River	Baltimore	138, 141
South	Baltimore	138, 141
Harvey	St. Mary's	110, 129
Hermitage	Dorchester	154
Herring Creek	Anne Arundel	119, 120
Hunting Creek	Calvert	124, 126
Island	Kent	115
Island	Talbot	143, 147
Kent Island, Lower	Talbot	143
King and Queen Parish, Upper	Charles	130
Langford's Bay	Kent	115
Leonard's Creek	Calvert	124, 126
Lyon's Creek	Calvert	124, 127
Manii (Monii)	Somerset	149, 150
Manokin	Somerset	149, 150
Mattapany	Somerset	149, 153
Middle Neck	Anne Arundel	119
Mill	Talbot	143, 147
Mount Calvert	Calvert	128
Nanjemy (Nanjemoy), Upper	Charles	130
Nanjemay (Nanjemoy), Lower	Charles	130
Nanticoke	Dorchester	154
Nanticoke	Somerset	149, 152
Newport	Charles	113, 130
New Town	St. Mary's	110, 111
Patapsco, North Side	Baltimore	138, 140
South Side	Baltimore	138
Pocomoke	Somerset	149, 151
Poplar Hill	St. Mary's	99, 110
Poquede Norton (or Bogettenorton)	Somerset	149, 153

INDEX

HUNDREDS	OLD COUNTY	
Portobacco, East Side	Charles	130
West Side	Charles	130
Resurrection	St. Mary's	110
Sassafrax, South	Cecil	158, 160
South River	Anne Arundel	119, 121
Specutia	Baltimore	138, 139
St. Clements	St. Mary's	111
St. Georges	St. Mary's	110
St. Inegos	St. Mary's	110
St. Maries	St. Mary's	110
St. Michaels	St. Mary's	110
Swan Creek	Kent	115
Town	Kent	115
Town Neck	Anne Arundel	119, 123
Tredhaven (Third Haven)	Talbot	143, 146
Tuckahoe	Talbot	143, 145, 146
West River	Anne Arundel	119, 120, 121
Wiccocomoco	Somerset	149, 152
William and Mary Parish, Upper	Charles	130
Lower	Charles	130
Worrell	Talbot	143
Worton	Cecil	158, 160

INDEX

ORIGINAL PARISHES

Parish	Present Name	Old County	
All Faiths	All Faiths	Calvert	108, 124, 125, 129
All Saints	All Saints	Calvert	108, 125, 127
Broad Neck	Westminster	Anne Arundel	108, 118, 119, *123*, 123
Christ Church	Christ Church	Calvert	108, *124*, 125, 129
Copley	St. John's	Baltimore	108, 138, 139, *141*, 141
Coventry	Coventry	Somerset	108, *151*, 151
Dorchester	Dorchester	Dorchester	108, 155, 157
Great Choptanck	Great Choptank	Dorchester	65, 108, *154*, 154, 155, *156*, 156
Herring Creek	St. James	Anne Arundel	108, 119, *120*, 120
King and Queen	King and Queen	St. Mary's	108, 111, 113, 130
Kent Island	Christ Church	Kent	108, 115, 116
Middle Neck	St. Ann's	Anne Arundel	108, 119, *122*, 122
Nanjemy	Durham	Charles	108, 131, 133, *134*, 134, 136
North Sassafrax	North Sassafras	Cecil	108, 109, 159, *160*, *161*, 161
Patapsco	St. Paul's	Baltimore	108, 118, 119, *137*, 138, 139, *140*, 140
Pickarnaxon	William and Mary	Charles	108, 131, *132*, 132, 133, 136
Piscattaway	St. John's	Charles	108, 119, *130*, 130, 131, *135*, 135, *136*, 136, 140
Portobacco	Portobacco	Charles	108, 131, *133*, 133, 136
Snow Hill	All Hallows	Somerset	108, 149, 153
Somerset	Somerset	Somerset	108, 148, *150*, 150
South River	All Hallows	Anne Arundel	108, 119, 120, 121
South Sassafrax	Shrewsbury	Cecil	108, 117, 159, 160, 161
Stepney	Stepney	Somerset	108, *152*, 152
St. Andrew's			109, 159
St. George's	St. George's	Baltimore	108, 115, *138*, 138, 139, 142
St. Michael's	St. Michael's	Talbot	42, 108, 143, 147
St. Paul's	St. Paul's	Calvert	108, 124, 125, 128
St. Paul's	St. Paul's	Kent	*15*, 108, *115*, 115, *117*, 117, *138*, 162
St. Paul's	St. Paul's	Talbot	108, 143, *144*, *145*, 145, *164*
St. Peter's	St. Peter's	Talbot	108, *143*, 143, *146*, 146
William and Mary	William and Mary	St. Mary's	108, 111, 112

Page numbers in *italics* denote reference to be found on illustration opposite the number

INDEX

LATER PARISHES

Parishes	Present Location	Old County	
All Saints	Frederick	Charles	*136*, 136
Chester	Kent	Kent	*114*
North Elk (or St. Mary Anne's)	Cecil	Cecil	*159*, 161
Prince George's	Prince George	Prince George	*130*, 135, *136*, 136
Queen Anne	Prince George	Prince George	128, *163*
Rock Creek	Dist. of Columbia	Charles	*130*
St. Luke's	Queen Anne's	Talbot	*144*, 145
St. Mary's White Chapel	Caroline	Dorchester	156
St. Thomas'	Baltimore	Baltimore	*139*, 140
Trinity	Charles	St. Mary's and Charles	129
Whitemarsh	Talbot	Talbot	146
Worcester	Worcester	Somerset	153
Wye	Queen Anne's	Talbot	145

Page numbers in *italics* denote reference to be found on illustration opposite the number

INDEX

CHURCHES

	OLD COUNTY	PRESENT COUNTY	
All Faiths	Calvert	St. Mary's	106, 129, *129*
All Hallows (Snow Hill)	Somerset	Worcester	153, *153*
All Hallows (South River)	Anne Arundel	Anne Arundel	106, 121, *121*
All Saints	Calvert	Calvert	127, *127*
All Saints (Monii)	Somerset	Somerset	42, 106, 150, *150*
All Saints (Frederick)	Charles	Frederick	136, *136*
Christ Church (Broad Creek)	Kent	Queen Anne's	12, 106, 116, *116*
Christ Church (Easton)	Talbot	Talbot	*143*, 146
Christ Church (Nanjemy)	Charles	Charles	*132*, 134
Christ Church, Cambridge	Dorchester	Dorchester	65, *156*, 156
Christ Church (I. U.)	Kent	Kent	*114*
Christ Church (Portobacco and La Plata)	Charles	Charles	106, *133*, 133
Christ Church (Wayside)	Charles	Charles	106, *132*, 132
Christ Church	Calvert	Calvert	106, *126*, 126
Christ Church (St. Michaels)	Talbot	Talbot	*143*, 147
Christ Church (Chaptico)	St. Mary's	St. Mary's	*113*, 113
Chester Church	Talbot	Queen Anne's	145
Coventry (Rehoboth)	Somerset	Somerset	*151*, 151
Emmanuel (Chestertown)	Kent	Kent	*114*
Middleham Chapel	Calvert	Calvert	*124*
Shrewsbury (Locust Grove)	Cecil	Kent	106, *160*, 160
Spring Hill	Somerset	Wicomico	152
Stepney (Green Hill)	Somerset	Wicomico	42, *152*, 152
St. Ann's (Middletown)	State of Delaware		161
St. Ann's (Annapolis)	Anne Arundel	Anne Arundel	*122*, 122
St. Andrew's (Princess Anne)	Somerset	Somerset	*148*
St. Andrew's (Leonardtown)	St. Mary's	St. Mary's	*111*
St. Clement's Manor	St. Mary's	St. Mary's	113
St. George's (Poplar Hill)	St. Mary's	St. Mary's	9, 13, 106, 112, *112*
St. James (Herring Creek)	Anne Arundel	Arundel	106, *120*, 120
St. John's (Broad Creek)	Charles	Prince George's	*135*, 135
St. John's (Kingsville)	Baltimore	Baltimore	106, *141*, 141
St. Luke's (Church Hill)	Talbot	Queen Anne's	106, *164*
St. Margaret's (Westminster)	Anne Arundel	Anne Arundel	*123*, 123
St. Martin's	Somerset	Worcester	*149*
St. Mary's (Northeast)	Cecil	Cecil	*159*
St. Paul's (Rock Creek)	Charles	District of Columbia	*130*
St. Paul's (Fairlee)	Kent	Kent	106, *117*, 117
St. Paul's	Baltimore	Baltimore City	*140*, 140
St. Paul's (Vienna)	Dorchester	Dorchester	*154*
St. Paul's (Baden)	Calvert	Prince George's	106, *128*, 128

Page numbers in *italics* denote reference to be found on illustration opposite the number

INDEX

CHURCHES

	Old County	Present County	
St. Paul's	St. Mary's		106
St. Stephen's (Earleville)	Cecil	Cecil	106, *161*, 161
St. Thomas (Garrison Forest)	Baltimore	Baltimore	*139*
Trinity (Church Creek)	Dorchester	Dorchester	106, *157*, 157
Trinity (St. Mary's City)	St. Mary's	St. Mary's	9, 106, *110*, 110
Trinity (Elkton)	Cecil	Cecil	*158*
Whitemarsh (ruins)	Talbot	Talbot	*146*, 146
Wye	Talbot	Talbot	106, *145*, 145
St. Paul's (Prince Frederick)	Calvert	Calvert	125, *125*
St. Paul's (Centerville)	Talbot	Queen Anne's	106, *145*, 145

Page numbers in *italics* denote reference to be found on illustration opposite the number

INDEX

GEOGRAPHICAL

Annapolis......... 19, 60, 63, 64, 67, 68, 93, 98, 99, 122, 134
Atlantic Ocean................ 153
Avalon, Newfoundland......... 3
Avon River.................... 134
Back Creek.................... 149
Baltimore City................ 140
Bermuda....................... 23
Blackwater River.......... 155, 156
Bodkin Point.............. 118, 137
Bohemia River................. 161
Brewer's Branch....... 145, 146, 147
Broad Creek............. 12, 116, 135
Broad Neck.................... 119
Bluff Point................... 113
Buck Neck..................... 114
Budd's (Bird) Creek........... 110
Bush River......... 13, 138, 141, 142
Calvert Town.................. 125
Cambridge............. 65, 154, 156
Centerville................... 145
Charlestown................... 159
Chesapeake Bay......... 5, 110, 112, 116, 117, 119, 120, 124, 137, 140, 141, 142, 147, 160, 161
Chester River 9, 115, 116, 117, 143, 145
Chestertown................... 115
Choptank River........ 143, 147, 148
Churn Creek................... 117
"Cloppers" (Colgate) Creek.... 140
Courte's Plantation........... 132
Cox Town...................... 127
Cresseye's Landing............ 132
Cresseye's Plantation......... 133
Delaware...................... 153
Dividing Creek................ 149
Dunn's Creek.................. 117
Eastern Bay............. 116, 143, 147
Eastern Shore.......... 145, 148, 154
Eastern Shore of Virginia..... 148
Easton................... 146, 147
Elk Neck...................... 141
Elk Ridge..................... 118
Elkton........................ 159
England...... 5, 7, 14, 16, 18, 19, 27, 33, 49, 73, 94, 102, 144
Fishing Creek................. 120
"Forked Neck" Plantation..... 147

France................49, 94, 102
Frederick (Maryland).......... 136
Gray's Inn Creek.............. 115
Green Hill.................... 152
Gunpowder River.......... 139, 141
Hambleton..................... 146
Hampton, Virginia............. 2
Head of Elk (Elkton).......... 159
Hell Point.................... 114
Hemsley's Plantation.......... 144
Herring Creek............. 118, 124
Hopton........................ 144
Hoskin's Quarter........... 133, 134
Hunt's Plantation.......... 155, 156
Indian Creek.................. 110
Ireland.............. 3, 49, 94, 102
Isle of Kent.............. 2, 6, 107
James River (Virginia)........ 12
Joppa.................... 138, 141
Judwin's Branch........... 145, 146
Kent Island...... 9, 12, 114, 115, 116
Kingsville.................... 141
Kipling, England.............. 3
Lambeth, England.............. 27
Langford's Bay................ 117
Langworth's Branch........ 111, 113
"Lisle Hall" Plantation........ 135
Little Choptank River...... 155, 156
London, England............ 14, 71
Longford, County of........... 3
Lyon's Creek.................. 120
Magothy River............. 118, 138
Manokin River............. 135, 138
Marston, England.............. 18
Maryland, Province of.. 1, 3, 6, 7, 15, 16, 18, 19, 23, 26, 27, 28, 29, 30, 31, 32, 35, 36, 47, 49, 93, 95, 96, 97, 102, 107, 109, 119, 130, 151
Mattawoman Creek....119, 113, 134
Middle River.......... 139, 140, 141
Middletown (Delaware)........ 161
Miles River Neck.............. 147
Monii......................... 150
Mt. Calvert............... 125, 128
Nanjemy.................. 133, 134
Nanticoke River............... 152
"Narrows," The........... 116, 143
New Castle (Delaware)......... 142

INDEX

GEOGRAPHICAL

New England.................. 1, 2
New Foundland............... 3
New Jersey..................23, 30
Newport....................... 113
New Town..................... 111
New Yarmouth................ 115
Ordinary Point................. 159
Oxford College................. 18
Oxford Town.................. 146
Palmer's Island............... 2
Patapsco River....118, 137, 138, 139
Patuxent River....110, 118, 120, 124
Patuxent River Main Road..... 111
Perryman..................... 142
Pettite's Old Field............. 140
Pine Hill Creek........110, 112, 124
Plowden's Wharf.............. 113
Pocomoke City............151, 153
Pocomoke River............... 151
Point Lookout.............110, 112
Poplar Hill.................6, 9, 112
Portobacco Creek.............. 113
Potomac River
    110, 130, 132, 133, 134, 135
"Prevent Danger" Plantation... 126
Princess Anne.............149, 150
Quantico..................... 152
Rehoboth, Maryland........... 151
Rock Creek................... 136
Sassafras River....109, 159, 160, 161
Severn Heights................ 123
Severn Ridge Path............. 127
Skipton Creek............144, 146
Snow Hill.................... 153
Spring Hill................... 152
State House (St. Mary's City).. 111
St. Clement's Bay..........112, 113
St. Clement's Island........... 6
St. Clement's Manor........... 113
St. Clement's River............ 111
St. George's................... 111
St. Mary's City
    2, 6, 15, 47, 49, 110, 121
St. Michael's.................. 147
Susquehanna River.......2, 137, 142
Swan Point................... 114
The "Three Notched Road"
    110, 112, 113, 124
Tred-Avon River.............. 147
Trent Creek.................. 129
Virginia..................1, 3, 6, 12
Waringtown................... 126
Watkin's Point................ 148
West Indies................... 5
Whitehall.........14, 18, 19, 23, 24
"White Plaines" Plantation.... 120
Wicomico..................... 113
Wicomico River..........113, 130
Windsor Castle................ 4
Worton Creek........114, 117, 160
Wye Mills.................... 147
Wye River................144, 147
Yorke........................ 144
Zachiah Branch............... 133
Zachias Swamp................ 113

INDEX

MISCELLANEOUS
Act "Concerning Religion," 1649 .... 10, 30
"For Maintainance of Ministers," 1661 12
"For the Service of Almighty God, Etc.," 1692 ... 10, 12, 15, 16, 17, 18, 47-58, 166
"For the Service of Almighty God, Etc.," Defining its purposes 87
"For the Service of Almighty God, Etc.," Defects of this Law 19
"For the Service of Almighty God, Etc.," Effective date 58
"For the Service of Almighty God, Etc.," Date Repealed 93
"For the Establishment of Religious Worship, etc.," 1702 .... 19, 71, 94
"For the Establishment of Religious Worship, etc.," Validity of 95, 96, 97
For Constables taking List of Taxables 59
Address to King William III.... 35
"Anabaptists" 11, 29, 30
Anglicans 6
Anglican Church 6
  Clergymen 6
  Faith 6
Answers to Queries about the Province, 1676 32
"Antinomian" 11
Assembly, Maryland Provincial 12, 13, 15, 16, 17, 19, 30, 40, 47, 48, 49, 58, 71, 73, 74, 93, 94, 101, 107
  Maryland Provincial, Changes in personnel 41, 42, 43
"Associators" 39
Appeals from Vestry decisions to be made to Governor and Council 91
Baptisms 25, 32, 65
"Barrowist" 11
Benefices, Collating of Ecclesiastical 17, 38
Bishop of London, Personal representative of 15
  Jurisdiction of the 12, 38

Board or Commissioners of Trade and Plantation 17, 23, 28, 30, 32, 71, 72
Book of Common Prayer 37, 71, 74, 100
Bray, Dr. Thomas..18, 19, 71, 73, 74
"Brownists" 11
Burials in the Province of Maryland 25, 32
Calverts, As Anglican Churchmen 14
  As Roman Catholics... 14
  Rule of terminated.... 14
  Rule of restored...... 14
Calvinists 11
Chaplains to the Council and Assembly 42
Charter of Avalon 3
  of the Province of Maryland 3, 4, 5, 9, 12, 14
Church of England... 1, 2, 3, 6, 8, 12, 15, 17, 18, 19, 26, 29, 30, 31, 36, 38, 47, 50, 71, 74, 75, 89, 93, 95, 99, 101
  Established by Law 15, 16, 51, 58, 93
  Growth of... 12
  Doctrines and discipline of the 17
  Rights, Liberties and Franchises of the... 15, 50
  Jurisdiction of the.... 15
  Governor Copley representative of the..... 15
  Rites of the. 17, 37
  Livings..... 12
Church, The Puritan........... 1
  The Roman Catholic... 1, 3
  "The Established"..... 75
Churches, Care of 65
  To be built in each Parish........... 17
  Twenty-two built in 1693............. 17
  Exceptions where churches are built.. 54

INDEX

MISCELLANEOUS

Churches, care of 65
    To be used for Court Houses............ 67
Church Wardens, Appointed each year........ 85
    Elected by Freeholders of the Parish.......... 85
    Oath of........ 85
    Fines for non-performance of duty..... 86
    To see that parochial charges are paid........ 86
    Fines to be levied by...... 86
Clerks of Parishes To make returns to County Courts.... 67, 68
    Fee for recording........ 52
Clerks of Parishes.............. 76
Colonies, The American........ 2
Colinists, The Roman Catholic.. 1
Commissary, Dr. Bray appointed 18
Commission of Gov. Lionel Copley........................ 14
Commonwealth of England..... 9
Copley, Instructions to Governor 16, 37
    Commission of Governor 14
    Representative of Crown and Church......... 15
Council, The King's, at Whitehall 14
Counties of the Province of Maryland............. 16, 108
    Work of Dividing into Parishes.......... 16, 51
County, Court Houses to be used as churches......... 64
    Seals................. 107
Decisions of Governor and Council Final................... 91
Disposition of the Forty per poll Tax....... 76, 98, 99, 100, 101, 102
Dissenters and Quakers exempted 92
Dissenters.................... 167
Drum, Council and Assembly called by beat of drum....... 42

Ecclesiastical Benefices........ 17, 38
England, The Great Seal of..... 14
    Revolution in......... 14
Fines To be applied to Parish uses.................. 53
    To be recorded in "Their Majesties' Names"..... 53
Freedom to worship God....... 2
Freeholders.................. 16, 51
    To be notified to attend meetings of Justices.......... 51
    Voters in church elections must be.... 78
    Vestrymen must be 79
    To name retiring vestrymen.......... 80
    To vote for church wardens......... 85
Glebes....................... 48
"Heretics".................... 11
"Idolators".................... 11
Inhabitants to furnish information...................... 81
"Independents".......... 11, 29, 30
Instructions to Governor Leonard Calvert and the Commissioners....................... 6, 7
Jesuit....................... 11
"Jesuited Papist"............. 11
Justices, Meeting of........... 51
    Jurisdiction of....... 87, 92
Laws of Province of Maryland repealed, 1692................. 44
Lord's Supper, Administering the 66
Lutherans.................... 11
Laws, Ecclesiastial of England.. 9
Lay Readers, Appointed in vacant Parishes... 65
    To assist ministers with two Parishes........... 65
    Appointed by Vestry............ 88
    Licensed by the Ordinary......... 88
    Salary of......... 88
    Oath and Licenses of............ 88
    Duty............ 89

INDEX

MISCELLANEOUS

Marriages, Prevention of Illegal. 76
   Who shall perform ceremony........... 77
   Fees............... 77
   Place and time of.... 77
   "Tables" to be provided............ 84
Meetings of Justices........... 53
Ministers of the Church of England............. 12, 13
   Expenses of transportation to Maryland. 18
   Induction of....... 15, 165
   Maintenance of 12, 16, 48, 75
   To be one of the Vestry 16, 48, 70
   Limited to two Parishes 88
Missionary............... 12, 13, 18
Oath of Governor and Council.. 8
   of Registrar............. 81
   of Vestryman........... 64, 79
      Additional.. 79
   of Church Warden........ 85
   Appointed by Parliament. 42, 80
"Papist-Priest"............... 11
Papists...................... 166
Parishes....... 16, 17, 24, 32, 48, 105
   Boundaires to be well defined... 15
   to be recorded in County Courts... 51
   Copy of Certificate to be sent Governor. 5
   Dividing Counties into. 16
   Number in each County 51
   Ratifying records of.... 83
Parochial Charges to be paid out of gifts to the Parishes....... 86
Penalties for Sabbath breaking.. 50
   for failing to carry out provisions of the Act of 1692............ 52
   for absence from Vestry meetings......... 84
Pilgrims of New England....... 2
   of the Province of Maryland............... 2

Places of Worship of Dissenters and Quakers to be registered.. 93
"Prespeterians"............. 11, 30
Protestants............. 7, 8, 9, 166
Protestant Governor........... 10
   Ministers........... 7, 9
   Revolution in the Province of Maryland......... 12, 14, 36
   Religion............ 36
Puritans...................... 1
Quakers............. 33, 92, 93, 166
Queries about the Province of Maryland.................. 29, 30
Registers of Parishes, Appointed. 81
   Oath of... 81
   To record vestry proceedings, etc. 81
   Fees...... 82
   To Furnish Copy of the Parish Records.... 90
   To Show Records of Parishes.. 82, 90
Religious Liberty............ 1, 5, 15
   An asset of the Calverts.... 5
   The "Child of Expediency" 15
Religious Toleration........... 8
Report to Governor and Council 16
Roman Catholics.3, 5, 6, 7, 8, 10, 14
"Romish Church"............. 29
"Roundhead"................. 11
St. Cecelia's Day.............. 5
St. George's Day.............. 111
Salaries of Chaplais.....n...... 42
"Scismatic".................. 11
"Separatists"................. 11
Sheriffs, Jurisdiction of......... 60
   To collect Forty per poll Tax............... 77
   To pay Forty per Poll Tax to Vestry....... 78
   Commission for collecting Tax............ 55

INDEX

MISCELLANEOUS

Sheriffs, Jurisdiction of 60
    To report Property Donations 66
    To report number of Taxables............ 66
    To collect additional Ten pounds Tax 87
    Fees................. 87
Sunday Observances 50
Tax, Forty pounds of Tobacco "per Poll" 16, 55
    Sheriff to Collect 55, 77, 87
    to pay to vestry 55, 77, 87
    How to be Spent.......... 56
    Application of remainder of 88
    Disposition of............ 76
    Ten pounds of Tobacco additional................ 87
    Sheriff's salary for collecting Taxables................... 66
    59
    List of Taxables kept with vestry records.. 55
Toleration Act 8
Trade Building in the Province of Maryland............... 24, 32
Vestries, Authority for 78
    Annual election on Easter Monday........... 80
    Authority for calling meetings........... 84
    To build churches and chapels............. 54
    To build churches where needed............. 64
    To determine dimensions of Churches and Chapels............ 54
    To obtain list of Taxables yearly......... 55
    Records to be kept in register............. 84
    To receive tax from Sheriff 55
    Instructed as to certain interior work on churches........... 63
    To see that churches are decently kept 57
    Meetings to be held once a month........... 83

Vestries, Authority for........... 78
    Public notice to be given of meetings.... 84
    Auhtorized to accept Donations.......... 56
    To act as a "Body Corporate"............ 57
    Authorized to sue..... 56
    To choose church wardens................ 64
    Meeting dates fixed.. 89
    Minimum constituting vestry............. 89
    Appeals from their decisions to be made to Governor and Council 91
    Authorizing vestry to Act................ 89
Vestrymen.................... 16
    Number constituting a vestry.......... 78
    Must be Freeholders. 79
    Oath of 64, 79
    Oath administered to First vestryman by one of the Justices. 79
    Oath administered to other vestrymen by First Vestryman... 79
    Additional Oath of.. 79
    Two new ones chosen annually......... 80
    Freeholders to name retiring vestryman. 80
    Penalty for absence from vestry meetings.............. 90
    Election of........ 53, 90
    Number of to be chosen.............. 53
    Given authority of office............. 53
    To fill vacancies.... 57, 78
    Suits to be entered in the name of the principal Vestryman............. 57
Virginia Colony, The......... 1, 3, 6
Visitation of Dr. Thomas Bray.. 19
Voters must be Freeholders..... 78
Whitehall, Council at.......... 19
Writs of Election of Burgesses... 41

INDEX

COUNTIES

Anne Arundel.. 39, 41, 106, 107, 108, 118, 119, 120, 124, 137, 140
Baltimore.. 39, 40, 106, 107, 108, 114, 118, 119, 137, 139, 141, 142
Calvert..... 39, 41, 96, 106, 107, 108, 112, 120, 124, 125, 127, 130
Cecil........... 39, 41, 42, 106, 107, 108, 109, 114, 115, 158
Charles........ 39, 41, 106, 107, 108, 113, 119, 124, 130, 131, 132, 133, 135, 138, 140
Dorchester.......... 39, 41, 65, 106, 107, 108, 154, 155, 156
Harford..................... 138
Kent........ 9, 39, 40, 106, 107, 108, 114, 115, 116, 158, 160, 165
Prince George's............ 124, 142
St. Mary's... 9, 39, 40, 106, 107, 108, 109, 110, 111, 112, 113, 124, 130
Somerset...... 39, 40, 41, 42, 43, 106, 107, 108, 148, 149, 150, 152
Talbot........ 39, 40, 41, 42, 43, 106, 107, 108, 143, 144, 146
Worcester.................... 149

COURT HOUSES

Anne Arundel County.......... 119	Dorchester................... 154
Baltimore.................... 138	Kent......................... 115
Calvert...................... 125	St. Mary's................... 111
Charles...................... 131	Somerset..................... 149
Cecil........................ 159	Talbot....................... 144

www.ingramcontent.com/pod-product-compliance
Lightning Source LLC
Chambersburg PA
CBHW061437300426
44114CB00014B/1718